Lecture Notes in Finance: Investments
Student Edition

Dr. David J. Moore

Revision 1: 2010.01.07

CONTENTS

3

What are you teaching students these days?

Imagine your finance professor having a beer at a bar in late 2008 as the economic crisis unfolded. A conversation between your professor and another patron arises. The other patron asks your professor "Oh, you are a professor, what do you teach?" I respond with "Investments" and other courses. Given the financial systems were apparently falling apart at that time, the next question was very apropos: "Investments? What are you teaching students these days?" At the time I responded with a simple "some combination of forgotten fundamentals and flawed fundamentals." Here, in this brief introduction to the course, is a more detailed response.

Fundamentals and assumptions

- Fundamentals

  - Higher risk, higher expected return
  - Equities outperform bonds due to higher risk of equities
  - Diversification, based on correlations, drives risk and return of portfolio
  - You can not time the market: index funds outperform actively managed forms, especially when factoring in fund costs and taxes

- Assumptions

  - Expected returns and risk are constant
  - Correlations are constant
  - Thus, what worked in the past shall work in the future

Challenges to fundamentals and assumptions

- The equity risk premium is overrated: U.S. Treasury bonds outperformed stocks over the preceding 10, 20, and 30 year periods and had about the same performance over the past 40 years[1]

    - I have been able to confirm this over the preceding 10 years when comparing 1-month treasury bills to monthly market returns. However stocks outperformed 1-month treasury bills over the preceding 20, 30, and 40 years. At some point in the future when I have free time, I will re-try using longer-maturity treasuries (which offer higher returns) or find a U.S. Treasury Bond index.

- 'We've never had a six-month period where we've lost 2 million jobs and the market has gained 50%" - Barry L Ritholz, CEO of FusionIQ [1]

    - True, but, we never had a population this large and thus never had so many people who *could* lose their job. Better to compare unemployment *rates* with market returns. Perhaps another study...

- "Interest rates are at zero, there's $2 trillion plus on the Federal Reserve's balance sheet, and yet the economy is still losing jobs... What exactly is the stock market romancing?" – Mohamed A. El-Erian, PIMCO CEO [1].

    - The current market P/E ratio (33) is roughly twice the historical average (16).

- "...the standard 60/40 stock/bond mix had almost a one-to-one correlation with the S&P500" [1].

    - The "diversified" stock/bond portfolio is *supposed* to have lower risk (standard deviation). A nearly one-to-one correlation with the riskier S&P500 does seem to imply the 60/40 portfolio will have the same standard deviation as the market. However, just because $\rho = 1$ that does not necessarily mean $\sigma_{60/40} = \sigma_{SP500}$.

Fundamentals that appear to remain valid

- Robert Muhlenkamp, a veteran fund manager [1]

  - September 2008: went 30% into cash and bought bonds in January 2009... allegedly did "everything textbooks suggested would avert disaster"
  - Has not outperformed the S&P500 over the past 3 years, in fact, he trailed by 3 points
  - 20 year client cashed out in March but phoned to get back in again in August after missing 50% market returns
  - I would argue the actions of Muhlenkamp and the client are actually *counter* to that in textbooks: you can not time the market but yet they tried to do so.

- "...some of the largest, savviest, and most influential pension funds in the world are lagging common stock market benchmarks..." [1]

- 2008 asset value of CalPERS plunged 23.4%, worse than the simple 60/40 portfolio [1]

- Jerry Goss, 27 year veteran of A.G. Edwards [1]

  - suggests "buy-and-hold is out" and "tactical asset management" is in (moving money to the sidelines when "warranted")
  - March 2009: moved 40% assets out of mutual funds and into commodities and international ETFs
  - Result: since Goss implemented the strategy in March 2009 (through October 2009) he has trailed the S&P500

- Sophisticated hedge funds "...were just two points better than the loss posted by a plain vanilla 60/40 stock/bond all location using inexpensive index funds."

  - Don't forget hedge funds charge high fees so that two point advantage is likely wiped out by the fees.

So now what?

- "New normal" asset allocation should include TIPS, commodities, and assets less correlated with the stock market

- Fundamentals of diversification still apply

- Fundamental of "don't time the market" sort-of applies with a caveat: expected returns, risk (variance), and correlations *do* vary over time, and this must be worked into some dynamic asset allocation strategy

- For now though, the 60/40, albeit sub-optimal, appears to be a good starting point for your retirement account

- Another thought: if we decide it is a bad idea to invest in the US, and invest our money overseas, what is going to happen here? We will continue to lose jobs. We need to invest in the US so that we can have jobs in the US.

- "The Capitalists will sell us the rope with which we will hang them." -V.I. Lenin. My application to the current scenario: China and India are selling us the rope (their "high growth" stocks) to hang us (by choking off investment in US companies, moving jobs overseas, etc.).

References

[1] Roben Farzad. Searching the stock market for the true north. *Business Week*, October 5th 2009.

Using These Lecture Notes

These lecture notes were prepared as a supplement, not a replacement, to the full text from Charles P. Jones entitled "Investments." Rather than use prepackaged terse PowerPoint slides and adhere to "artificial" constraints I have collected my notes in this document. The Lecture Notes follow the text closely with references to the text in the form of (9e), (10e), or (11e) that reference the 9th, 10th, and 11th edition of the text, respectively. A cross-reference to the relevant Charles P. Jones "Investments" text is provided at the beginning of each chapter in these Lecture Notes.

In addition, to facilitate classroom interaction and to encourage reading the full text, significant pieces of information have been intentionally left out of these lecture notes. For instance, worked out numerical examples are typically not found in these lecture notes but are discussed in-class and written on the pseudo-old-fashioned whiteboard. Also, you will find many unanswered questions throughout these notes which will be asked of you, the student, to answer during class. Thus, reading the notes before class will not only better prepare you for the lecture, but can make you appear as a superstar armed with answers to all of my questions.

Thank you for purchasing this text. Now, lets get to work and hopefully some day soon our work and our joy will be indistinguishable.

-David J. Moore, Ph.D.

Part I

Overview of Investments

Why: Study of Investments (chapter 1 10e/11e)

1.1 Key concepts

- Understand why return and risk are important considerations of *all* investing decisions

- Scope of investment decisions

- Investment decision process

1.2 Nature of investments

- Investments (the commitment of funds) could be in financial assets (paper assets) or real assets (gold, real estate, human capital)

- Some investments are marketable securities (easily and inexpensively traded financial assets)

- A *portfolio* is the collection of securities held by an investor

- We invest to make money

1.3   The importance of studying investments

1.3.1   Wealth impacts

See Table 1-1 (9e), Example 1-1 (10e, 11e)

1.3.2   Career options

Investment banker - can make millions of dollars arranging the sale of new securities, facilitating mergers and acquisitions, and leveraged buyouts. (mention recent trip to New York and comments from multiple people about stressed out investment bankers)

Bond traders - can make \$200k $\rightarrow$ \$750k depending on experience trading bonds.

Security analyst - \$200k $\rightarrow$ \$500k, prepare research reports on companies for public corporations or institutions (e.g., valuation of a firm for possible merger or acquisition)

Portfolio manager management investments to achieve risk-return goals of client. Typically make on the order of 1% of assets under management.

Stock broker - 80,000 registered brokers today. Average pay \$100k per year. Median is \$63k. What does this mean?

Financial planner 2/3 of affluent Americans use a financial planner. (1) I'll be part of the other 1/3, (2) These folks are too busy making the money too worry about investing it. Again, charge on the order of 1% .

1.4   Investment decision process

1.4.1   Basis of decisions

Expected return *ex-ante* return expected by investors over some period of time (for a given amount of risk)

Realized return *ex-post* (actual) return on an investment

Risk $Pr[\text{expected} - \text{actual}] \neq 0$. Some may define it as $Pr[\text{actual} < 0]$

Risk averse investor investor who prefers less risk to more risk. More importantly, must be induced (compensated) for taking on additional risk

Risk/return tradeoff : See Figure 1-1 (9e, 10e, 11e)

1.4.2 The decision process

Individual security analysis valuation of individual securities (which includes expected cash flows, risk, and expected return

Portfolio management the analysis of the interactions of a collection of investment assets (Intel and Dell move together, Intel and Philip Morris do not)

Passive investment strategy buy and hold

Active investment strategy make changes to proportions of available investment assets over time

Efficient market hypothesis markets are efficient and as a result securities are priced correctly (story of two people walking down the street and seeing $20 bill).

1.5 Considerations for today's investors

1.5.1 Uncertainty

Current value is the discounted future earnings. Earnings are estimates, discount rate is an estimate.

1.5.2 Global investments

This change from Figure 1.1 to Figure 1.2 illustrates the importance of diversification. However, some of my cursory analysis (and some other academic results) have shown the diversification benefits are not that great. Q: Why not?

1.5.3 Old vs. New economy

I wish I ignored this talk and stuck with what I learned in school

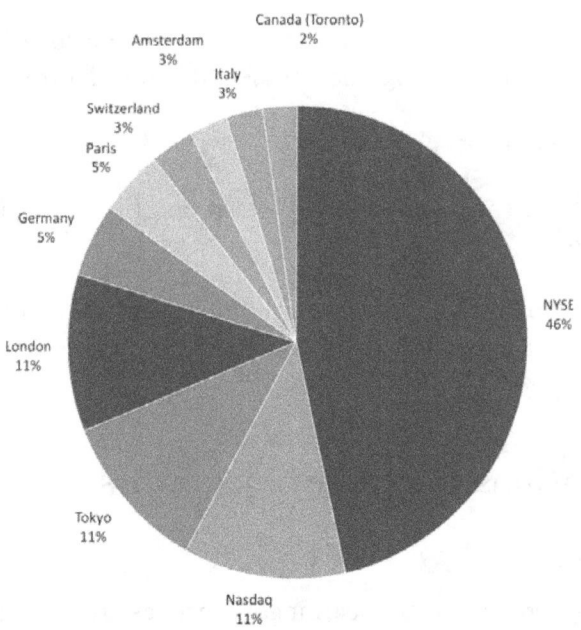

Figure 1.1: US and World market capitalizations (1998)
Source: World Federation of Exchanges

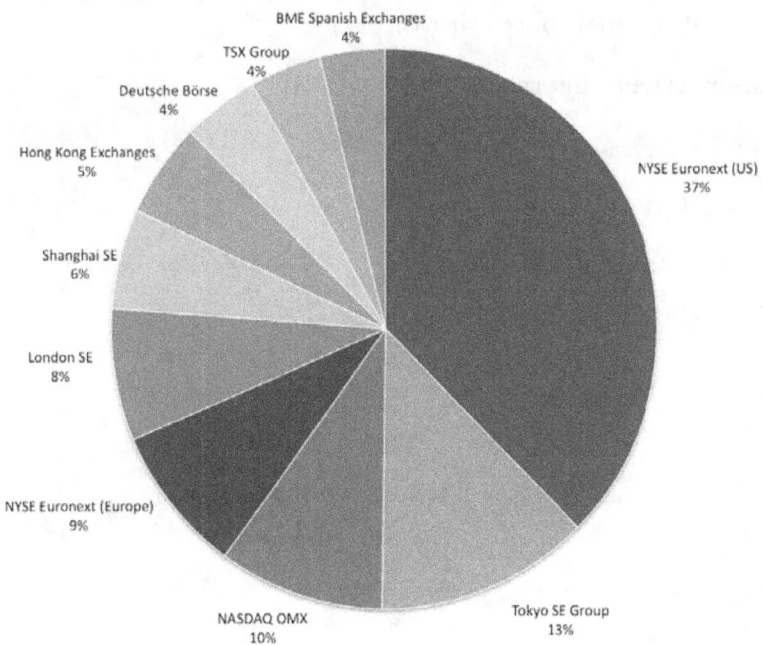

Figure 1.2: US and World market capitalizations (2008)
Source: World Federation of Exchanges

1.5.4   Rise of the Internet

Information availability, transaction cost reduction, search cost reduction

1.5.5   Institutional investors

- Includes pension funds, mutual funds, bank trust departments, and insurance companies

- Pension $\rightarrow$ 401k: A trend that began in the 1990s. Essentially transfers risk (think about optimal contracting theory)

- Regulation FD and Internet

TWO

What: Direct Investments (chapter 2 10e/11e)

2.1 Key concepts

Stocks, bonds, options, futures

2.2 Organizing financial assets

See Exhibit 2-1 (9e, 10e, 11e)

Direct investments - buy and sell yourself

Indirect investments - underlying securities are bought and sold on your behalf. Easiest example: international mutual funds. A lot easier than opening bank and brokerage accounts in foreign lands and trading on their markets.

2.3 Non-marketable securities

1. Examples are given in exhibit 2-1

2. What is non-marketable? A financial asset for which there is no market.

3. Liquidity: the ability to buy or sell easily with minimal price effects

4. non-marketable does not necessarily mean illiquid. For instance, savings accounts are non-marketable but you can cash out at any time.

5. Important non-marketable financial assets

   (a) Savings account - typically pay very little interest

   (b) Non-negotiable CDs

   (c) Money market deposit accounts - higher interest, still FDIC insured. note: you may have to tell your bank to "sweep" funds in order to get the higher interest rate

   (d) Savings bonds - according to Malkiel, not a good deal. Perhaps these are less important unless you are patriotic and want to "take it for the team (country)".

2.4   Money market securities

1. What is the "money market": The market(s) for short-term, liquid, low-risk financial assets (T-bills, negotiable CDs, etc.)

2. T-Bill: short term (less than 6 month) instrument sold by government at a discount. Two ways to compute returns.

   (a) Investment yield:

   $$IY = \left(\frac{\text{face value} - \text{purchase price}}{\text{purchase price}} \right) \times \left(\frac{365}{\text{maturity in days}} \right)$$

   (b) Discount yield: used by government to quote but not by us.

   $$IY = \left(\frac{\text{face value} - \text{purchase price}}{\text{face value}} \right) \times \left(\frac{360}{\text{maturity in days}} \right)$$

2.5   Fixed income securities

What is fixed?

2.5.1   Bonds

Long term (> 1 year) debt instrument

Par value (*face value*) - amount returned to you at maturity

Coupon periodic interest paid by issuer

Zero-coupon bonds - pays no coupons. How do you get a return? Sold at a discount. Malkiel aptly points out how this eliminates reinvestment rate risk. More on this later

Call provision ability of issuer to repay face value and cease coupon payments. Why keep paying you 10% when I can issue new bonds at 5%?

2.5.2 Types of bonds

Treasury bonds - risk free

TIPS Treasury inflation-indexed securities

1. bond *value* adjusts with inflation (CPI).
2. Taxes due each year on interest (coupon) and inflation adjustments (change in value)

Agency securities aggregated and securitized mortgages, student loans, farm credit, etc.

Municipal securities state and city bonds (could be issued to build new roads, construct hospitals, or shore up budget shortfalls → think California). Note risk will vary and interest is exempt from federal taxes.

$$\text{taxable equivalent yield} = \frac{\text{Tax-exempt municipal yield}}{1 - \text{marginal tax rate}}$$

Example: Say $T = 28\%$ is the marginal tax rate and $Y = 5\%$ is the municipal yield. Therefore the TEY is:

$$TEY = \frac{Y}{1 - T} = \frac{0.05}{1 - 0.28} = 6.94\%$$

Also note that some municipal bonds are also exempt from state taxes. In these cases you compute the effective state rate first:

$$\text{effective state rate} = \text{state marginal tax rate}(1 - \text{fed tax marginal tax rate})$$
$$= 0.10(1 - 0.28) = 7.2\%$$

Note: this is less than 10% because what you pay in state taxes are tax deductions from your marginal tax rate. Then compute the combined tax rate:

$$\text{combined tax rate} = \text{effective state} + \text{marginal tax rate}$$
$$= 7.2 + 28 = 35.2\%$$

Now compute the TEY:

$$TEY = \frac{0.05}{1 - 0.35} = 7.7\%$$

Corporate bonds again, to obtain cash to fund projects

1. Bonds are *senior securities* (senior to preferred or common stock in the event of liquidation)

2. There are different levels of security associated with a bond. *Debentures* are not backed by assets, rather, they are backed by the issuer's overall financial soundness.

3. Direct access notes (DANs) - issued at par with no accrued interest. Typically for buy and hold investors and marketed (sold) direct from issuer to purchaser

4. Can be convertible

5. bond ratings - letters assigned by rating agencies such as Standard and Poor's and Moody's to reflect the relative probability of default. See exhibit 2-4

6. junk bonds - low-grade (BB or lower) with higher yields. Sometimes referred to as "high-yield bonds"

2.5.3   Asset backed securities

- What are they? Securities issued against asset-linked debts bundled together. A result of *securitization*: bunch if illiquid loans → liquid ABS

- Further examples - check out example 2-7 in book (includes tax liens, electric bills, and even delinquent child support payments)

2.6 Equity securities

Thus far we have talked about securities with fixed payment amounts and dates (with one exception, can anyone tell me? TIPS). Now on to equity securities where, as we all know, there only thing fixed is change (and even then the rate of change varies).

2.6.1 Preferred stock

Really a hybrid between fixed-income and equity securities.

1. pays fixed dividend known in advance

2. unlike bonds, company is *not* legally required to pay dividends and will *not* be in default if it fails to pay

3. **cumulative dividends** if dividends can not be paid, unpaid dividends must be paid in the future *before* common stock but *after* debt obligations

4. **non-cumulative dividends** - in the event of omitted dividends, preferred stock holders may be allowed to vote for board of director members (you didn't pay my dividends, I'll vote you out of there)

5. has a claim on liquidation value *after* debt holders but *before* stockholders (and has an associated par value)

2.6.2 Common stock

1. Represents ownership interest in a company

2. stockholders are also referred to as residual claimants (what is left after fixed income claims)

3. par value - can be anything

4. book value - value of shareholder's equity. Okay, who remembers the balance sheet equation from accounting? Assets = Liabilities + shareholder's equity

5. dividends - quarterly cash payments from corporation to the shareholder. Should the payment of dividends affect stock price?

6. dividend yield - dividends / stock price

7. payout ratio - dividends / earnings

8. Example 2-10

   (a) Coke decides on May 24 (**declaration date**) that dividends will be paid on July 2 (**payment date**)

   (b) At the same time Coke declares the **holder of record date** to be June 7

   (c) The brokerage industry sets the **ex-dividend date** to be June 5. On or after this date purchasing stock will *not* entitle you to the July 2 dividend. The difference between *holder of record* and *ex-dividend* dates is a result of the time needed for a stock purchase to "settle" - checkout wikipedia

   (d) dividend will be mailed to stockholders of record (communicated to Coke by brokerage industry?)

9. stock dividend - pay shares of stock instead of cash

10. stock split - your one share is now two shares (book value per share is now 1/2)

11. P/E ratio - price to earnings ratio

12. ADRs - American depository receipts - a means to purchase foreign stock on U.S. exchanges

2.7   Derivative securities

Definition: securities whose value is *derived* from another security

1. Option - a right (option) to buy or sell at a specified price within a specified period

   (a) put - option to sell

   (b) call - option to buy

   (c) LEAP - longer maturity option (up to 2.5 years) - as in leap of faith

2. Warrant - option *created by the corporation* to purchase a stated number of shares at a specified price at a specified time in the future (typically several years)

3. Futures contract - *agreement* to exchange in the future at a specified price. no initial cash outlay.

What: Indirect Investments (chapter 3 10e/11e)

3.1 Key concepts

1. Why is indirect investing important?

2. What is the difference between UITs, closed-end funds, and open-end funds?

3. Open-end (mutual) fund concepts - sales charges, management fees, NAV

4. What are ETFs?

3.2 Does anyone use mutual funds?

1. 50% of U.S. households in 2003 (and this was after the dotcom bust), roughly 95 million people

2. 1/3 hold mutual funds in employer-sponsored plans

3. > 1/3 hold funds outside employer-sponsored plans

3.3 Investing indirectly

1. Pay an investment company to buy portfolio for you

2. Receive pro-rata share of dividends, capital gains, and interest

3. Pay pro-rata share of fees (which result from transaction costs, advertising expenses, employee pay, etc. - this will come in later when discussing cost efficiency)

3.4   What is an "investment company"

1. A financial company that sells shares of *itself* to the public and uses these funds to invest in a portfolio of securities

2. Regulated investment companies *can* elect to pay no federal taxes on dividends, interest, and realized capital gains. In this case shareholders pay taxes at their marginal tax rate.

3. To be qualified as a regulated investment company:

   (a) 90% of income from securities

   (b) 90% of taxable income distributed to shareholders

   (c) $\leq 25\%$ in any one security

   (d) some other strange 50%/5% rule

4. What is an example of an *unregulated* investment company?

3.5   Types of investment companies

1. UITs - unit investment trusts

   (a) unmanaged - holds a basket of securities and mix does not change

   (b) funds must be left in UIT until maturity date

   (c) very small part of investment company assets

2. Closed-end investment company

   (a) fixed capitalization (funds raised from IPO only, no new additional shares are created or sold)

   (b) shares are traded

   (c) market price may be at premium or discount of NAV

3. Open-end investment company (aka mutual funds)

    (a) variable capitalization (new shares created when money flows in, shares disappear when money flows out)

    (b) Shares are not traded. Rather, they are bought and sold between investment company and investor

4. NAV: See Example 3-8 (10e), Example 3-6 (11e)

3.6 Major types of mutual funds

1. Money market fund

    (a) open-ended investment company that invests in money market instruments

    (b) unlike money market *deposit accounts*, money market *funds* are <u>not</u> insured.

2. stock funds and bond funds

    (a) Morningstar style box: See Figure 3-4 (10e), Exhibit 3-2 (11e)

    (b) large, mid, small represent market capitalization

    (c) Value is for dividend paying stocks (typically), growth is for capital appreciation (hoping for stock price appreciation) and blend is somewhere in between

3.7 Mechanics of investing indirectly

1. closed-end funds: why does NAV differ from market price? No agreed upon answer, lets move on.

2. open-end funds

    (a) may have front-end load (sales fee), back-end load (redemption fee), or no-load

    (b) Class A: front end load, lower distribution (12b-1) fee and annual expenses (I've got your money upfront, no need to pick away at you in the future)

    (c) Class B: back end load that declines over time. If held long enough, converts to Class A (which has lower distribution fees)

    (d) Class C: No front end load, smaller back-end load than B, back-end loan fixed indefinitely, does not convert to Class A

    (e) Example of different loads: See Example 3-12 (10e), Example 3-10 (11e)

3. no-loads are a result of no sales force (see comments on fund supermarkets later)

4. My advice: no-load; studies have shown funds with lower fees are more efficient and therefore have better performance Q: How can you connect lower fees with better performance?

3.8   Investment company performance

1. Total return = cumulative return

2. Average annual return = geometric mean

3. Morning star ratings are a function of

    (a) relative risk in category

    (b) return *history* (not a guarantee of future returns)

    (c) management fees

    Note: a rating of 5 stars today does not guarantee a rating of 5 stars next year.

4. Benchmark - used to compare performance with a *comparable* investment. Typically an index such as the S&P500 (large cap) or Russell 2000 (small cap)

5. Are expenses important? As aforementioned, higher fees are correlated with inefficient portfolio management. Over a 5 year period (not sure which one):

    (a) Top 25 funds had 207% *total* return and fees of 1.09%

    (b) Bottom 25 funds had 26% total return and fees of 3.25%

6. Performance consistency

    (a) Index funds have lower expenses (Q: why) and have outperformed 2/3 of all actively managed funds since 1976

    (b) What about the other 1/3? No way to know in advance which funds will be in this 1/3, even the fund managers themselves likely did not know.

3.9 International indirect investing

I talked earlier about how costly it would be to invest in foreign securities. A few naming conventions:

1. International fund - primarily <u>non-US</u> securities

2. Global fund - $\geq 25\%$ in US securities

3. Single-country - primarily closed end (or ETFs)

4. ADRs are another means of investing in foreign securities. Not sure if there is a mutual fund that invests solely in ADRs.

3.10 ETFs

1. ETFs are index funds that trade like stocks

2. Can be bought on margin and sold short (unlike open-end funds)

3. Examples include "Spiders", iShares, Cubes, etc.

4. Mechanics are setup such that $NAV \approx$ market price see the footnote in the book

5. Tax efficient - typically little or no capital gains distributions since funds are indexed (i.e., passively managed). Also, when someone sells shares, the mutual fund does not have to liquidate in order to pay. Rather, shares are exchanged on the market.

6. Summary of differences between open-end, closed-end, and ETFs:

Characteristic	Open	Closed	ETF
traded?	No	yes	yes
NAV,mkt value	$=$	$\neq$	$\approx$
management	active/passive	active	passive
tax efficiency	less	less	more

3.11   Future of indirect investing

1. Fund supermarkets - use Schwab, Fidelity, Etrade, etc., to choose among thousands of mutual funds

2. Managed accounts - high net worth individuals may choose to pay a fund manager $\leq 2\%$ of assets to manage their money

3.12   Hedge funds

1. unregulated - therefore disclose little about investing practices

2. require substantial investment

3. invest in derivatives, use leverage, and use illiquid assets unavailable to mutual funds

4. take a percentage of profits, typically 20% or more

Where: Securities Markets (chapter 4 10e/11e)

4.1 Distinguish between primary vs. secondary markets

See Figure 4.1 (10e, 11e).

- IPOs - first time issuance, "seasoned" not the first time

- note which is primary and which is secondary market

- Investment banking

- shelf rule dollar cost averaging

- lowest cost bidder $\rightarrow$ one who will pay the most per share and charge the least fees

- illegal laddering vs. legal "stabilization" (stabilization: if all is not sold in first day (i.e., not fully subscribed) can legally place purchase orders at a fixed price)

- private placement (angel investors e.g. Andy Bechtolsheim of Cisco): saves time and money by not registering however securities are not marketable (because they are not registered). Non marketable -> more risk -> higher yield required

4.2 Where equities, bonds, and derivatives are traded

- Equity securities - NYSE, Amex, Nasdaq, regional exchanges, OTC, ECNs

- Bonds - OTC, NYSE and AMEX bond markets (with relatively small amounts of corporate bonds)

- Put and call options - several options exchanges (e.g., CBOE)

- Futures contracts - various futures exchanges (CME)

4.3   Equity market organization

4.3.1   Definitions

broker intermediary who represents both buyers and sellers and attempts to obtain the best price possible for either party. Income source: commissions.

member (NYSE, AMEX): any firm (or individual) that owns 1 or more seats

seat NYSE has 1366 seats (and number has been fixed for several decades)

- cost $< \$100k$ in 1970s and \$1.5M in 3/03
- ML owns 20 seats
- seat market ceased at the end of 2005

specialist (NYSE, AMEX): a member who is charged with maintaining an orderly market in one or more stocks by buying or selling for his or her own account

dealer (Nasdaq, OTC): an individual firm who makes a market in a stock by buying from and selling to investors. Income source: spread between bid and ask price

"make a market" post bid and ask prices and align buyers and sellers

4.3.2   Stock exchanges

Some NYSE filing requirements:

- $\geq 40M$ market cap

- 1.1M common shares

- specific amounts of net tangible assets

- and others

For more information on NYSE, brokers, and specialists, see exhibit 4-3 on page 91 of the text.

Table 4.1: Summary of Stock Exchange Distinctions

Item	NYSE	AMEX	Nasdaq	OTC	ECN
type	organized exchange	organized exchange	network of dealers	network of dealers	computerized trading network
securities	only NYSE	only AMEX (options ant ETFs)	Nasdaq, AMEX, and NYSE	Not listed on any organized exchange or market	Nasdaq
# of firms					
listing costs	higher	lower	?	?	0
trading mechanism	auction market, specialists act as both broker and dealer	auction market, specialists act as both broker and dealer	dealers buy and sell securities from and to investors	dealers buy and sell securities from and to investors	matches buy and sell orders from their own subscribers and orders routed from other brokerage firms

4.3.3 ECNs / in-house trading

- Income source is commissions (about 1c per share).

- No spreads and no conflicts of interest with the broker. In essence, you are your own dealer.

- In-house trading: between fund manager's at a given firm. For example, Fidelity in-house trades account for 5-10% of NYSE trading volume.

- Nasdaq trading: As of August 2002, ECNs account for 45%, Nasdaq market 30%, in-house brokerage order matching 25%

- NYSE trading: 85% NYSE, 10% in-house, 5%?

Additional info on ECNs

- In order to trade on ECN you must be a subscriber

- Schwab routes ECN orders through UBS which displays and executes orders through NYSE Arca

- Allows for 24/7 trading potential (although Schwab's ECN orders are available pre-market and after hours only). Why?

4.4 Stock market indexes

- DJIA Price weighted index of 30 leading *industrial* stocks

- S&P500: Value-weighted (market-cap) index

- Let μ = mean monthly return

- $H_0 :$ $\mu_{djia} = \mu_{sp500}$ can not be rejected

- $\rho_{sp,nyse,djia} \approx 0.90$

- a representation of "the market"

- indexes exist for all sorts of asset classes

4.5 Bond Markets

- Treasury bonds: initial purchase from federal reserve then traded

- Agency bonds: Fannie Mae

- Municipal bonds: How 'bout those California munis? From 1/2008 to 8/2008 only municipal bonds had non-negative returns (WSJ)

- Corporate bonds: GM, Ford anyone?

How: Trading Mechanics (chapter 5 10e/11e)

5.1 Brokers' roles and brokerage firm operation

5.1.1 Types of brokerages

Full-service broker A brokerage firm offering a full range of services including information and advice. Merrill Lynch

Discount broker A brokerage firm offering execution services at prices typically significantly less than full-service (full line) brokerage firms. Schwab

Online discount brokers E*Trade, ScottTrade, TD-Ameritrade

Interesting fact at the beginning of 2003 there were 62 discount brokers who offered trading online. Of that 62, 37 were primarily on-line firms.

5.1.2 Types of brokerage accounts

Account type	Description
Cash	all securities purchases are made with cash; leftover cash is typically placed in money-market instruments (book uses "asset management account" designation). Commissions paid per trade
Margin	Securities can be purchased "on credit." Same commission structure as cash account
Wrap	All costs are wrapped into one annual percentage fee. May or may not have private money manager (typically 2%)

5.1.3 Investing without a broker

Type	Description
DRIP	Dividend reinvestment plan. The company (say IBM) uses dividends to buy additional shares (either full or fractional). Can even have money withdrawn periodically from bank account to purchase shares
DSPP	Direct stock purchase plan. Make initial purchase from company at 0-7c per share. Raises capital without underwriting fees
Treasury Direct	Can buy or sell Treasuries by the phone or Internet directly from the government

5.2 Changes in the securities business

5.2.1 Brokerage firms

- Full-service → discount → online → discount with online operations

- Decrease in fees: Interesting fact: commission fees have dropped from 25c/share in 1975 to a few cents a share for exchange-listed stocks.

5.3 How orders to buy and sell securities work

5.3.1 NYSE (exchange) mechanics

5.3.1.1 Basics

1. investor places order at brokerage firm

2. brokerage firm transmits order to NYSE trading floor

3. Common Message Switch/SuperDot transmits order to broker's booth or to specialist

4. Floor broker takes order to the trading post, competes for the best price, and makes the trade

5. Report is sent back to originating brokerage firm

5.3.1.2 Automation of the NYSE

SuperDot bypass broker's booth, order sent directly to trading post, report sent back to member firm via SuperDot as well

OARS helps specialist set opening price based on pre-opening orders

A dot mechanism for anonymous trading. Why would you want to do this?

5.3.1.3 Decimalization of stock prices

Before decimalization, stocks traded in eighths and sixteenths. This enabled a spread of at least one-eighth of a point (12.5c per share). After decimalization, the average NYSE spread is currently around 1 cent.

5.3.2 Nasdaq (market) mechanics

1. investor places order at brokerage firm

2. firm forwards order to one of several market makers (Nasdaq averages 11 per security)

3. dealers are constantly buying and selling so they complete the trade and earn the spread

4. report sent back to originating firm

5.4   Different types of orders

Checkout this website http://www.sec.gov/answers/orderbd.htm

5.4.1   Definitions

Order type	Definition	Actual trade price (S_t)
Market	buy or sell order to be executed by the broker immediately at current market prices	S_t
Limit	buy a security at no more (or sell at no less) than a specific price (S_l)	For buy limit: $S_t \leq S_l$ For sell limit: $S_t \geq S_l$
Stop	buy or sell a stock *once the price of the stock reaches a specified price*, known as the stop price (S_s) . When the specified price is reached, the stop order is entered as a market order.	$S_t \approx S_S$ Actual trade price can vary widely to the betterment (detriment) of investor.
Stop-limit	Once the stop price (S_s) is reached, the stop-limit order becomes a limit order to buy or to sell at no more (or less) than a specified price (S_l)	For buy stop-limit: $S_l \geq S_s, S_t \leq S_l$ For sell stop-limit: $S_l \leq S_s, S_t \geq S_l$

A few examples...

5.4.2 Execution options

Execution	Description
Day	Execute entire order today or cancel
Fill or Kill	*Entire* order should be executed immediately or it should be canceled
Good 'Til cancel	Order to buy or sell a security which remains in effect until executed or canceled
Immediate or cancel	Order should be executed all *or in part* immediately or it should be canceled
Do not reduce	Instructs the broker not to reduce your limit price by the amount of the cash dividend when a stock goes ex-dividend and the market price is reduced by the amount of the dividend

5.5 Investor protection

SEC Setup in 1934 to protect investors via

- Information disclosure regulation

- Investment companies regulation

- Regulation of firms or individuals who sell advice

- Insurance via ???

NASD A self-regulating body but still under SEC authority.

5.6 Margin trading

Type	Definition
Actual margin (AM)	amount of holdings that is not borrowed from the broker $AM = \frac{\text{current value of securities - amount borrowed}}{\text{current value of securities}}$
Initial margin (IM)	part of a transaction customer must pay to initiate transaction (transaction implies initiate)
Maintenance margin (MM)	Percentage of a security's value that must be on hand as equity (maintenance implies you already own the security)
Margin call (MC)	A demand from the broker for additional cash or securities as a result of the actual margin declining below the maintenance margin $MC \text{ price} = \frac{\text{amount borrowed}}{\text{number of shares}(1 - \text{MM})}$

Note: $MM < AM < IM$.

A few examples...

5.7 Short selling

Short sale: the sale of a stock not owned but borrowed in order to take advantage of the expected decline in the price of the stock.

1. Investor believes IBM is overpriced at $60. Investor does not own IBM.

2. Issue short sale of 100 IBM shares

3. Brokerage borrows from another investor's account (or borrows from a fund within the firm or enters a long position themselves and lends the shares to you)

4. Securities are sold and investor receives $6000.

5. Investor must put up 50% of the borrowed amount (IM). Investor is now responsible for paying back 100 shares of IBM.

6. If lender of shares wants the shares back (i.e., closes their long position) the broker either borrows the shares elsewhere or borrower's short position will be closed out (i.e., require borrower to return shares which they must obtain by purchasing first). If stock price falls to $40 three months later the investor is up

$2,000. (Buy 100 shares @ 40 and replace the 100 shares borrowed) - closed out short position nets $2,000.

Overview of Portfolio Management (chapter 21 10e/11e)

6.1 Key concepts

- Portfolio management is a process

- How to apply the process to various investment situations

- Asset allocation

6.2 The portfolio management process

- The process applies to both passive (indirect investment via index funds) and active (direct investment in individual securities) strategies

- The process can be simplified into 5 steps

  1. Specify objectives, constraints, and preferences of the investor
  2. Asses current market expectations
  3. Develop strategy (asset allocation) and implement
  4. Periodically measure actual performance and compare with objectives
  5. Repeat 1-4 periodically (aka, portfolio revision)

- Q: Why repeat periodically?

- Individual vs. institutional portfolio management

	Individual	Institutional
Risk	"Losing money"	standard deviation
Constraints	less resources	more regulated
Taxes	important for non-retirement accounts	less important
Policy revision	more frequent	less frequent

6.3 Investment policy formation

6.3.1 Objectives

- Individual investor life-cycle approach: a means of establishing return requirements and risk tolerance. See Figure 21-2 (10e, 11e)

- "Ignoring the Great Depression, which hopefully will not occur again..." Q: Any comments?

- Do not forget inflation: at 3% inflation, the purchasing power of a dollar drops in half in less than 25 years. You'll be hurting if you ignore inflation, retire at 60, and live to 85+.

6.3.2 Constraints and preferences

Time horizon Retirement vs. home purchase in 5 years; short-term institutional fund vs. long-term

Liquidity needs How likely are you to need invested funds in the short-term? Should you invest in CDs or purchase rental property?

Tax considerations how much to invest in IRAs/401ks/529s vs. regular brokerage accounts; for institutional managers, tax-managed vs. non-tax managed strategy

Legal or regulatory requirements applies more to institutional investors, especially with the broadness of the "Prudent Man Rule": managers shall act like people of prudence, discretion, and intelligence

Unique circumstances e.g., a trust fund that has specific investment activities or assets

6.4 Capital market expectations

- Form expectations based on Macro (bond market, stock market, business cycle, etc.) and Micro (Porter's five forces, accounting statement analysis, etc.) conditions

- Rate of return assumptions: "past is prologue" but remember no one has a 100% accurate crystal ball. You could apply Monte Carlo simulation techniques to, say, asset allocation.

6.5 Implementing the investment strategy

- Up to this point we have: target risk/return, constraints, and market expectations "in the toolbox"

- Now build the proper asset allocation, which is the most important factor affecting return and risk

- Can use life-cycle approach, Schwab guidelines, web-calculators, etc.

- Portfolio optimization: use index funds for each asset class

6.6 Monitor

- Asses current market expectations

- Asses any changes in investor circumstances

- Asses any new "financial innovation"

6.7 Rebalance

- In general, a rebalanced portfolio is less volatile than one that is not

- An example...

- Problem: you are selling winners than may continue to win and buying losers that may continue to lose

- But...: what goes up must come down (and vice versa)

- Could also consider some form of CPPI

- Buetow, Sellers, Trotter Hunt, and Whippler (2002) - The Benefits of Rebalancing

    - Study of two-asset case (equity and fixed income)
    - Rebalancing can add value
    - Daily rebalancing when allocation is off by 5% or more performed best
    - Futures can be used to reduce the cost
    - Conclusions are consistent with Plaxco and Arnott (2002)

Part II

The Mathematics of Investing

Individual Security Return and Risk (chapter 6 10e/11e)

7.1 Key concepts

4 things you should know by the end of the chapter

1. Calculation of return and risk of financial assets

2. key terms - geometric mean, cumulative wealth index, inflation-adjusted returns, currency adjusted returns

3. Historical returns on major financial assets

4. Estimating future returns and risk

7.2 Return

7.2.1 Components of return

Two components to return

- yield = income component

- capital gain (loss) = change in stock price of a security over time

A few examples...

7.2.2 Measuring return

Total return Typically applied to an individual security, measures the "total return" which includes the yield component and capital gain component.

$$TR = \frac{(P_1 - P_0) + CF}{P_0} \tag{7.1}$$

Note that total return may be positive or negative.

Relative return It is often to convenient to express return as a relative measure, hence the name relative return:

$$RR = \frac{P_1 + CF}{P_0} \tag{7.2}$$

Q: Can anyone relate RR to TR? Q: What is the minimum value of RR?

Cumulative wealth index Yet another measure of return is the cumulative wealth index which measures the ending wealth given a beginning value:

$$CWI_n = WI_0 \prod_{i=1}^{n} (1 + TR_i) = WI_0 \prod_{i=1}^{n} (RR_i) \tag{7.3}$$

Foreign investments The TR of a US investment in a foreign company is calculated by:

$$TR_{US,F} = \left(RR \frac{USF_1}{USF_0} \right) - 1 \tag{7.4}$$

where USF = US dollar amount of 1 unit of foreign currency.

An example...

7.2.3 Summary statistics for returns

There are two measures of average return: arithmetic mean and geometric mean. The arithmetic mean is calculated as:

$$\overline{X} = \frac{1}{n} \sum_{i=1}^{n} X_i \tag{7.5}$$

The geometric mean is calculated as:

$$G = \left(\prod_{i=1}^{n} RR_i \right)^{1/n} - 1 \qquad (7.6)$$

Arithmetic mean is typically used to estimate future returns (statistically, it is an unbiased estimator) and Geometric mean is used to measure the realized compound rate of return.

A quick example... Thus far we have talked about nominal returns. While nominal returns indicate changes in dollar amounts, they do not consider the purchasing power of those dollars. Insert inflation adjusted returns (aka real returns):

$$TR_{IA} = \frac{1 + TR}{1 + IF} - 1 \qquad (7.7)$$

where IF is the rate of inflation

7.3 Risk

The dispersion of returns is often referred to as risk. In this section we discuss factors that contribute to this dispersion and how to measure risk.

7.3.1 Components of risk

Interest rate risk sensitivity of a firm's returns to fluctuations in interest rates (if you are financed with ARMs or credit cards or lines of credits)

Market risk sensitivity of firm's returns to fluctuations in the market (fluctuations in market risk premium)

Inflation risk sensitivity of a firm's returns to fluctuations in inflation (fluctuations in prices of inputs)

Business risk industry-specific risk

Financial risk more debt financing = more risky

Liquidity risk how soon can security be bought or sold

Exchange rate risk sensitivity of firm's returns to fluctuations in exchange rates
Country or political risk - is the government stable?

In general, risk is classified into two types of risk

Systematic risk attributable to broad macroeconomic factors affecting all securities

Nonsystematic risk attributable to factors unique to the security

7.3.2 Measuring risk

The dispersion of returns is typically measured using the variance (square of the standard deviation) calculation:

$$\sigma^2 = \frac{1}{n-1} \sum_{i=1}^{n} \left(X - \overline{X}\right)^2 \qquad (7.8)$$

Technically, this is the unbiased estimate of population variance. In reality, we form an estimate of the *population* variance using just a *sample* of data. In that case, replace $1/n-1$ with $1/n$.

Another measure of risk is the **risk premium**. Risk premium is the additional compensation for assuming risk. A form of risk premium is the **equity risk premium**, the difference between the return on stocks and the risk free rate. There are a number of ways to calculate the equity risk premium.

- The book's ERP measure:

$$ERP = \frac{1 + G_{CS}}{1 + G_{RF}} - 1 \qquad (7.9)$$

where G_{CS} is the geometric mean return on common stocks, i.e., "the market."

- Simple difference:

$$ERP_{simple} = E\left[R_{CS}\right] - R_F \qquad (7.10)$$

7.4 A note on historical returns

Although you will not be able to predict returns with 100% accuracy, relative relationships are unlikely to vary significantly. See Table 6-6 (10e, 11e).

Wait a second. I thought Treasuries were associated with the risk-free rate. Why is there measurable risk?

EIGHT

Portfolio Return and Risk (chapter 7 10e/11e)

8.1 Key concepts

- Understand the meaning and calculation of expected return and risk measures for an individual security

- Recognize what it means to talk about modern portfolio theory

- Understand portfolio return and risk measures as formulated by Markowitz

- Understand what the efficient frontier is and its importance to investment analysis.

8.2 Uncertainty

- Realized returns = past returns that you have observed

- Expected return = best estimate of future return

8.2.1 Probability Distribution

An example... Q: what is the area under the curve?

8.2.2   Calculating expected return for a security

The expected rate of return is the arithmetic mean

$$E[R] = \frac{1}{n} \sum_{i=1}^{n} R_i \tag{8.1}$$

8.2.3   Calculating risk for a security

Three types of variance based on whether or not you have observed the entire population (N) or just a sample of the population (n):

1. Input: Population, Output: Population variance

$$\sigma^2 = \frac{1}{N} \sum_{i=1}^{N} \left(X - \overline{X} \right)^2$$

2. Input: Sample, Output: Sample variance

$$s_n^2 = \sigma^2 = \frac{1}{n} \sum_{i=1}^{n} \left(X - \overline{X} \right)^2$$

3. Input: Sample, Output: unbiased estimate of *population* variance

$$s^2 = \frac{1}{n-1} \sum_{i=1}^{n} \left(X - \overline{X} \right)^2 \tag{8.2}$$

We will primarily use (8.2) and call it σ^2.

8.3   Portfolio return and risk

Consider a portfolio with n securities. Let the percentage of a portfolio invested in security i be represented by the portfolio weight w_i. Note $0 \leq w_i \leq 1$. Q: what does this mean? . Therefore

$$\sum_{i=1}^{n} w_i = 1$$

8.3.1 Portfolio return

The expected return on a portfolio p can be calculated as:

$$E\left[R_p\right] = \sum_{i=1}^{n} w_i E\left[R_i\right] \tag{8.3}$$

An example...

8.3.2 What portfolio risk is not

Portfolio risk can not be calculated by simply taking a weighted average of individual risks:

$$\sigma_p^2 \neq \sum_{i=1}^{n} w_i \sigma_i^2 \tag{8.4}$$

But this is a good thing. In reality, the portfolio's risk will be less.

8.4 Analyzing portfolio risk

If all securities have the same risk $\sigma_i^2 = \sigma^2$, and this risk are independent of each other, then the standard deviation of the portfolio is given by:

$$\sigma_p = \frac{\sigma}{n^{1/2}} \tag{8.5}$$

In reality, everything is related to some extent, so such a simple formula can not be used.

8.4.1 Diversification

Diversification is a key to managing risk. The simplest diversification is called random or naive diversification. This is accomplished by randomly picking securities for what is available. See Figure 7-2 (10e, 11e).

8.5 Modern portfolio theory

The inequality in equation (8.4) is due to relationships between the movement of stocks. Therefore, modern portfolio theory (MPT) is essentially the derivation of a measure of portfolio risk that accounts for: 1. weighted individual security risks 2. weighted co-movements between securities returns

8.6   Measuring co-movements in security returns

8.6.1   Correlation coefficient

The *relative* relationship between co-movements of returns of returns is measured by the correlation coefficient ρ. The value of ρ is bounded by +1.0 and -1.0 with:

$$\rho = \begin{cases} +1.0 & \text{perfect positive correlation} \\ 0 & \text{no correlation} \\ -1.0 & \text{perfect negative correlation} \end{cases}$$

Nothing is perfect. Q: Intel / Dell positive or negative? American airlines and Exxon?

8.6.2   Covariance

The *absolute* measure of co-movement is called covariance σ_{AB}. Covariance of two securities on an expected return basis is calculated as:

$$\sigma_{AB} = \sum_{i=1}^{n} \left(R_{A,i} - \overline{R}_A \right) \left(R_{B,i} - \overline{R}_B \right) pr_i$$

Covariance and correlation are related in the following manner:

$$\rho_{ij} = \frac{\sigma_{ij}}{\sigma_i \sigma_j}$$

8.7   Calculating portfolio risk

8.7.1   Two-security case

For the two-security case, portfolio risk σ_p is calculated as:

$$\sigma_p^2 = w_1^2 \sigma_1^2 + w_2^2 \sigma_2^2 + 2 w_1 w_2 \rho_{12} \sigma_1 \sigma_2 \tag{8.6}$$

An example...

8.7.2 The n-security case

In general,

$$\sigma_p^2 = \sum_{i=1}^{n} w_i^2 \sigma_i^2 + \sum_{i=1}^{n} \sum_{\substack{j=1 \\ i \neq j}}^{n} w_i w_j \sigma_{ij}$$

$$= \sum_{i=1}^{n} \sum_{j=1}^{n} w_i w_j \sigma_{ij}$$

$$= \sum_{i=1}^{n} \sum_{j=1}^{n} w_i w_j \rho_{ij} \sigma_i \sigma_j$$

Therefore three variables determine portfolio risk:

1. individual variances

2. Covariances

3. Weights

Note: as the number of securities increases, the importance of each securities variance decreases. Q: Why?

8.8 Markowitz portfolio model

The set of portfolios generated by the Markowitz portfolio model, i.e., *feasible* portfolios obtained by varying w_i and w_j in:

$$E\left[R_p\right] = \sum_{i=1}^{n} w_i E\left[R_i\right]$$

$$\sigma_p^2 = \sum_{i=1}^{n} \sum_{j=1}^{n} w_i w_j \sigma_{ij}$$

8.9   Optimum portfolio weights

To find the weights of a two asset portfolio that minimizes the variance, begin with the variance of returns of:

$$
\begin{aligned}
V[R_P] &= V[x_A R_A + x_B R_B] \\
&= V[x_A R_A] + V[x_B R_B] + 2Cov[x_A R_A, x_B R_B] \\
&= x_A^2 \sigma_A^2 + x_B^2 \sigma_B^2 + 2 x_A x_B \sigma_{AB}
\end{aligned}
$$

Substitute $x_B = 1 - x_A$:

$$
\begin{aligned}
\sigma_P^2 &= x_A^2 \sigma_A^2 + (1 - x_A)^2 \sigma_B^2 + 2 x_A (1 - x_A) \sigma_{AB} \\
&= x_A^2 \sigma_A^2 + \left(1 - 2x_A + x_A^2\right) \sigma_B^2 + 2 \left(x_A - x_A^2\right) \sigma_{AB} \\
&= x_A^2 \left(\sigma_A^2 + \sigma_B^2 - 2\sigma_{AB}\right) - 2 x_A \left(\sigma_B^2 - \sigma_{AB}\right) + \sigma_B^2
\end{aligned}
$$

Take the partial derivatives and set equal to zero:

$$
\frac{\partial \sigma_P^2}{x_A} = 2 x_A \left(\sigma_A^2 + \sigma_B^2 - 2\sigma_{AB}\right) - 2 \left(\sigma_B^2 - \sigma_{AB}\right) = 0
$$

$$
x_A = \frac{\sigma_B^2 - \sigma_{AB}}{\sigma_A^2 + \sigma_B^2 - 2\sigma_{AB}}
$$

$$
\begin{aligned}
x_B &= 1 - x_A \\
&= \frac{\sigma_A^2 + \sigma_B^2 - 2\sigma_{AB}}{\sigma_A^2 + \sigma_B^2 - 2\sigma_{AB}} - \frac{\sigma_B^2 - \sigma_{AB}}{\sigma_A^2 + \sigma_B^2 - 2\sigma_{AB}} \\
&= \frac{\sigma_A^2 - \sigma_{AB}}{\sigma_A^2 + \sigma_B^2 - 2\sigma_{AB}}
\end{aligned}
$$

NINE

Optimum Portfolio Selection (chapter 8 10e/11e)

9.1 Key concepts

1. appreciate the importance of the efficient frontier

2. understand how an optimal portfolio of risky assets is determined

3. apply the Markowitz optimization procedure

4. recognize the single-index model

5. understand how the total risk of a portfolio can be broken into two components

9.2 Building a portfolio using Markowitz principles

The Markowitz technique for optimal portfolio selection has two steps

1. Identify optimal risk-return combinations from available risky assets

2. Choose final portfolio from efficient frontier based on investor's risk preferences.

The Markowitz portfolio selection model (how investors should act to diversify) is based on three assumptions:

A1 Single investment period

A2 No transaction costs

A3 Preferences based only on expected return and risk

9.2.1   Individual utility

Efficient Frontier The set of portfolios generated by the Markowitz portfolio model.

Indifference Curves Curves describing investor preferences for risk and return

Risk Averse If given a choice, you will not take a fair gamble (gamble that has equal probabilities of gain or loss).

9.2.2   Generating the efficient frontier

Given the following inputs:

- estimates of expected return for each security (n estimates)
- estimates of risk for each security (n more estimates)
- correlation of securities (some more estimates)

a computer program varies portfolio weights until the return is maximized for a given level of risk.

9.2.3   A note on international diversification

International diversification can reduce risk. However, in recent years, the correlation has increased. For instance, in 1992 $\rho_{us,eafe} = 0.58$ and in 2002 $\rho_{us,eafe} = 0.91$. Q: why? However, the correlation is less between *smaller* foreign companies, emerging market companies, and U.S. firms.

9.2.4   Summary of the Markowitz model

1. A two-parameter model (expected return and risk)

2. Portfolios on the efficient frontier are equally "good"

3. Does not incorporate risk-free assets

4. Model input estimation varies

5. Model is cumbersome. As n increases, the number of required estimates increases according to:

$$\text{number of estimates} = \frac{n(n+3)}{2} \qquad (9.1)$$

Elaborating on (9.1), lets look at the number of estimates required for a 3 security case. The var-covar matrix is:

$$\begin{bmatrix} \sigma_{11} & \sigma_{12} & \sigma_{13} \\ \sigma_{21} & \sigma_{22} & \sigma_{23} \\ \sigma_{31} & \sigma_{32} & \sigma_{33} \end{bmatrix}$$

However, we know $\sigma_{ii} = \sigma_i^2$ and $\sigma_{ij} = \sigma_{ji}$. Therefore:

$$\begin{bmatrix} \sigma_1^2 & \sigma_{12} & \sigma_{13} \\ \sigma_{12} & \sigma_2^2 & \sigma_{23} \\ \sigma_{13} & \sigma_{23} & \sigma_3^2 \end{bmatrix}$$

Finally, the number of estimates required for the Markowitz model includes 3 variances, 3 covariances, and 3 expected returns for a total of 9 estimates.

9.3 Alternative methods of obtaining the efficient frontier

9.3.1 Excel solver

9.3.2 Single index model

1. Estimate β and α by relating all returns to a single market index:

$$R_i = \alpha_i + \beta_i R_M + e_i \qquad (9.2)$$

where

$$R_i = \text{return of security } i$$
$$R_M = \text{return of market index}$$
$$\alpha_i = \text{part of security } i\text{'s return independent of market performance}$$
$$\beta_i = \text{constant which measures how } R_i \text{ changes with } R_M$$
$$e_i = \text{random error (residual)}$$

2. Estimate individual security variance by

$$\sigma_i^2 = \beta_i^2 \sigma_M^2 + \sigma_{ei}^2 \qquad (9.3)$$

where σ_{ei}^2 is the residual variance from (9.8).

3. Estimate covariance by

$$\sigma_{ij} = \beta_i \beta_j \sigma_M^2 \tag{9.4}$$

4. Estimate portfolio beta as

$$\beta_p = \sum_{i=1}^{n} w_i \beta_i \tag{9.5}$$

5. Estimate portfolio variance as

$$\sigma_p^2 = \beta_p^2 \sigma_M^2 + \sigma_{ep}^2 \tag{9.6}$$

The total number of estimates required for the SIM is $3n + 2$. 3 for β, 3 for α, 1 for β_p and 1 for σ_p.

9.3.3 Multi-index model

Say you have strong convictions about another component of a firm's return other than just the overall market return (e.g., the particular industry's return). Insert the multi-index model:

$$R_i = \alpha_i + b_i R_M + c_i NF + e_i \tag{9.7}$$

where NF is a non-market factor.

9.3.4 Which performs better

In theory one might expect the MIM to outperform the SIM since it has the potential for more explanatory power (and therefore smaller error terms). However, there is no conclusive evidence on which is better. However, Cohen and Pogue (1967) found:

- *ex-post* performance of index models (SIM and MIM) are <u>not</u> dominated by Markowitz formulation → okay to estimate using SIM and MIM to save computing time and resources from an *ex-post* perspective

- *ex-post* performance of MIM is not superior to SIM. → okay to use SIM if only considering *ex-post* estimation

- efficient sets (generated either by Markowtiz, SIM, or MIM) dominate random portfolios and are not dominated by mutual funds → better to use SIM or MIM than randomly select stocks or choose a mutual fund

- *ex-ante* Markowitz is better than SIM, SIM is better than MIM (see figure 1 of Coehn and Pogue 1967)

Finally, regarding the number of estimates required, look at the following comparison between single-index and Markowitz:

n	Markowitz $(n(n+3))/2$	single index $3n+2$
2	5	8
3	9	11
4	14	14
5	20	17
6	27	20
7	35	23
8	44	26
9	54	29
10	65	32
100	5,150	302
200	20,300	602
300	45,450	902
4,000	8,006,000	12,002

9.4 The asset allocation decision

Asset Allocation Decision The allocation of a portfolio's funds to classes of assets, such as cash equivalents, bonds, and equities. Some major asset classes include: U.S. stocks, foreign developed markets, foreign emerging markets, government bonds, corporate bonds, T-bills, treasury inflation protected securities (TIPS), and real estate investment trusts (REITs). Table 8-1 of the text illustrates several asset allocation schemes including the associated portfolio weightings and risk return profile.

Note studies have determined that more than 90% of the investment return is explained by asset allocation decisions (Ibbotson and Kaplan 2000). See Table 8-1 (10e, 11e).

9.5 Appendix: Exploring the Efficient Frontier

Three different approaches to generating the efficient frontier are examined in this document. The efficient frontier is plotted with portfolio risk on the x-axis (σ_p) and expected portfolio return on the y-axis ($E[R_p]$). At each point on this graph, return is maximized for a given level of risk, or equivalently, risk is minimized for a given level of return.

9.5.1 Constructing the efficient frontier

9.5.1.1 Markowitz model

The equations for expected portfolio return and portfolio variance are as follows:

$$
\begin{aligned}
E[R_p] &= \sum_{i=1}^{n} w_i E[R_i] \\
\sigma_p^2 &= \sum_{i=1}^{n}\sum_{j=1}^{n} w_i w_j \sigma_{ij} \\
&= \sum_{i=1}^{n}\sum_{j=1}^{n} w_i w_j \rho_{ij} \sigma_i \sigma_j
\end{aligned}
$$

To obtain $(\sigma_p, E[R_p])$ points for the efficient frontier, the following estimates are needed:

1. n estimates of individual security expected return ($E[R_i]$)

2. n estimates of individual security variances (σ_i^2)

3. $n(n-1)/2$ unique covariances (σ_{ij}), or correlation coefficients (ρ_{ij}) if you prefer

   (a) Begin with variance-covariance matrix which has $n \times n = n^2$ entries

   (b) Subtract n from this number since the main diagonal will *not* be covariances, rather, they will be variances ($\sigma_{ii} = \sigma_i^2$). Now we have $n^2 - n = n(n-1)$ covariances

   (c) The covariances are symmetric ($\sigma_{ij} = \sigma_{ji}$) therefore only half of the remaining covariances are needed (are unique) leaving $n(n-1)/2$ unique covariances

Therefore, the total number of estimates required is:

$$
\begin{aligned}
\# &= n + n + \frac{n(n-1)}{2} \\
&= \frac{4n + n^2 - n}{2} \\
&= \frac{n^2 + 3n}{2} \\
&= \frac{n(n+3)}{2}
\end{aligned}
$$

As an example, consider the number of estimates required for a 3 security case. The variance-covariance matrix is:

$$
\begin{bmatrix}
\sigma_{11} & \sigma_{12} & \sigma_{13} \\
\sigma_{21} & \sigma_{22} & \sigma_{23} \\
\sigma_{31} & \sigma_{32} & \sigma_{33}
\end{bmatrix}
$$

However, we know $\sigma_{ii} = \sigma_i^2$ and $\sigma_{ij} = \sigma_{ji}$:

$$
\begin{bmatrix}
\sigma_1^2 & \sigma_{12} & \sigma_{13} \\
\sigma_{12} & \sigma_2^2 & \sigma_{23} \\
\sigma_{13} & \sigma_{23} & \sigma_3^2
\end{bmatrix}
$$

Therefore, in the three security case, the number of estimates required for the Markowitz model includes 3 variances, 3 covariances, and 3 expected returns for a total of 9 estimates:

$$
\# = \frac{3(3+3)}{2} = \frac{3(6)}{2} = 9
$$

9.5.1.2 Single index model

The equations for expected portfolio return and portfolio risk are as follows:

$$
\sigma_p^2 = \beta_p^2 \sigma_M^2 + \sigma_{\epsilon p}^2
$$

$$
E\left[R_p\right] = \alpha_p + \beta_p E\left[R_M\right]
$$

where

$$
\begin{aligned}
\beta_p &= \text{portfolio beta} \\
\alpha_p &= \text{portfolio alpha} \\
\sigma^2_{\epsilon p} &= \text{variance of portfolio error term} \\
\sigma^2_M &= \text{variance of market return} \\
E\left[R_M\right] &= \text{expected market return}
\end{aligned}
$$

To obtain $(\sigma_p, E\left[R_p\right])$ points for the efficient frontier, the following estimates are needed

1. Expected market return

$$
E\left[R_M\right] = \frac{1}{T} \sum_{t=1}^{T} R_{Mt}
$$

2. Market variance

$$
\sigma^2_M = \frac{1}{T-1} \sum_{t=1}^{T} \left(R_{Mt} - E\left[R_M\right]\right)^2
$$

3. Portfolio alpha (α_p), beta (β_p), and error term variance $\left(\sigma^2_{\epsilon p}\right)$ as computed from individual security estimates.

   (a) For each individual security, estimate α_i, β_i, and ϵ_i by relating all returns to a single market index:

$$
R_i = \alpha_i + \beta_i R_M + \epsilon_i \tag{9.8}
$$

   where

$$
\begin{aligned}
R_i &= \text{return of security } i \\
R_M &= \text{return of market index} \\
\alpha_i &= \text{portion of security } i\text{'s return independent of market performance} \\
\beta_i &= \text{constant which measures how } R_i \text{ covaries with } R_M \\
\epsilon_i &= \text{random error (residual)}
\end{aligned}
$$

(b) Assume portfolio is constructed with weights w_i. Therefore, the portfolio return is:

$$
\begin{aligned}
R_p &= \sum_{i=1}^{n} w_i R_i \\
&= \sum_{i=1}^{n} w_i \left(\alpha_i + \beta_i R_m + \epsilon_i \right) \\
&= \left(\sum_{i=1}^{n} w_i \alpha_i \right) + \left(\sum_{i=1}^{n} w_i \beta_i \right) R_m + \left(\sum_{i=1}^{n} w_i \epsilon_i \right) \\
&= \alpha_p + \beta_p R_M + \epsilon_p
\end{aligned}
$$

where

$$
\begin{aligned}
\alpha_p &= \sum_{i=1}^{n} w_i \alpha_i \\
\beta_p &= \sum_{i=1}^{n} w_i \beta_i \\
\epsilon_p &= \sum_{i=1}^{n} w_i \epsilon_i
\end{aligned}
$$

(c) The portfolio error term variance is computed as

$$
\sigma_{\epsilon p}^2 = \frac{1}{T-2} \sum_{t=1}^{T} \hat{\epsilon}_{pt}^2
$$

Therefore, the total number of estimates required for the SIM is $3n + 2$:

1. n estimates of β_i (1 for each security)

2. n estimates of α_i (1 for each security)

3. n estimates of ϵ_i (1 for each security)

4. market expected return: $E\left[R_M\right]$

5. market variance: σ_M^2

9.5.1.3   Excel solver

Using excel's solver function, you need just two estimates: portfolio expected return and portfolio standard deviation. To generate the efficient frontier:

1. open the alternativeFrontier.xls file

2. Start Excel's solver feature (Tools $\rightarrow$ Solver)

3. Select a target portfolio risk value (say $\sigma_p = 7$) and add/modify the constraint

4. Run solver and note the results:

   (a) portfolio weights
   (b) portfolio expected return
   (c) portfolio standard deviation

5. Repeat 2-4 and increment the target portfolio risk value

When complete, you will have points $(\sigma_p, E[R_p])$ to plot the efficient frontier. Note this technique is based on just two estimates (expected return and risk) and utilizes excel's solver feature to find the efficient combinations (weights) that result in the efficient frontier.

9.5.2   Concluding remarks

The primary distinction between the Markowitz model and the Single-Index Model is the Markowitz model requires calculations of individual security covariances (σ_{ij}) whereas the single index model is only concerned about covariance relative to the market (β_i). Therefore, with the Markowitz model, estimates of security i's covariance with n other securities must be calculated. With the single index model, only one covariance is needed for security i: the covariance with respect to the market.

In all three approaches the efficient frontier is computed by maximizing return for a given level of risk or minimizing risk for a given level of return by adjusting weights of individual assets (w_i). The approaches differ only in the method of estimating expected return and risk.

Relationship Between Risk and Return (chapter 9 10e/11e)

10.1 Key concepts

1. Understand capital market theory as an extension to portfolio theory

2. Understand the CML, SML, and relationship to portfolios and securities

3. Understand CAPM is used to equate the required rate of return

4. Understand APT

10.2 Capital Market Theory

CMT is a set of predictions concerning equilibrium expected returns. It is based on some simplifying assumptions:

1. All investors can borrow or lend money at R_F

2. Investors have homogeneous expectations based on expected return, variance of returns, and correlations

3. All investors have the same one-period time horizon

4. No transaction costs

5. no taxes

75

6. no inflation

7. no single investor can affect the price of a stock

8. capital markets are in equilibrium

It is important to note that although these assumptions may seem unrealistic, a true measure of a model's worth is its explanatory power.

All models are wrong, some are useful

Introduction of the risk free asset   Q: What is a risk free asset?

10.3   The capital market line

Capital Market line: The tradeoff between expected return and risk for efficient portfolios. Instead of RF, A, and B, the CML is the straight line when applied to the Markowitz efficient portfolio. Now for a picture...
   Q: Derive CML equation from the graph:

$$E[R_P] = R_F + \frac{E[R_M] - R_F}{\sigma_M}\sigma_P \tag{10.1}$$

An example...

Market portfolio: The portfolio of all risky assets
   Under CMT, all investors will hold some combination of the risk free asset and the market portfolio. Q: Why?

Separation theorem: The idea that the decision of which portfolio of risky assets to hold is separate from the decision of how to allocate investable funds between the risk-free asset and the risky asset.

10.4   The security market line

The CML represents the risk/return tradeoff for combinations of risk free asset and efficient portfolio. The SML represents the risk/return tradeoff for individual securities or inefficient portfolios.

Beta: A measure of a security's risk *relative* to the market.
   Draw a graph of market return vs. security return

1. x-axis: market return

2. y-axis: security return

3. 45 degree line represents beta $= 1$

CAPM: Capital asset pricing model. Relates the required rate of return for a security given its level of risk as measured by beta.
   Draw another graph of the SML:

1. x-axis: beta

2. y-axis: required rate of return (k_i)

3. zero beta $=$ zero risk $\rightarrow R_F$

Note the required rate of return is the risk free rate plus a risk premium. Derive fundamental CAPM equation by taking slope of the line:

$$k_i = R_F + \beta_i(E[R_M] - R_F)$$
$$E[R_i] = R_F + \beta_i(E[R_M] - R_F) \qquad (10.2)$$

An example...

10.5   Estimating SML (CAPM)

Market Model   Linear relationship between the return on each stock to the return on the market. The SML (collection of $\beta/E[R_i]$ relationships, is often estimated using standard OLS regression:

$$R_i = \alpha_i + \beta_i R_M + \epsilon_i \qquad (10.3)$$

   In this model, the total return measurement is used. Because all models are wrong and some are useful, observations will be observed above and below the fitted line.

10.6 Tests of CAPM

The conclusions are of CAPM are sensible:

1. Return and risk are positively related - greater risk should carry greater return

2. The relevant risk for a security is a measure of its market (systematic) risk

An obvious question is: how well does the model match reality? Extensive research has been done, both by academics and by practitioners, and there is some consensus on conclusions:

1. SML appears to be linear

2. The intercept term is generally higher than RF

3. The slope of CAPM is generally less steep than posited by the theory

4. No persuasive case has been made that nonsystematic risk commands a risk premium. That is the ratio of risk/return is not better for a highly risky company and therefore investors are rewarded only for assuming systematic risk.

10.7 Arbitrage Pricing Theory

APT can be viewed as a superset of CAPM. Under APT, equilibrium market prices will adjust to eliminate any arbitrage opportunities. An arbitrage opportunity arises to a situation where a zero investment portfolio can be constructed to yield a risk-free profit.

APT does not assume (unlike CAPM)	APT *does* assume (like CAPM)
A single-period investment horizon	Investors have homogeneous beliefs
The absence of taxes	Investors are risk-averse utility maximizers
Borrowing and lending at the rate RF	Markets are perfect
Investors select portfolios on the basis of expected return and variance	Returns are generated by a factor model

10.7.1   The model

The APT model assumes investors believe asset returns are generated randomly according to a n-factor model:

$$R_i = E[R_i] + \beta_{i1} f_1 + \beta_{i2} f_2 + \cdots + \beta_{in} f_n + e_i \qquad (10.4)$$

where

$$R_i = \text{the actual (random) rate of return on security } i \text{ in period } t$$
$$E[R_I] = \text{expected return of security } i$$
$$f = \text{the deviation of a systematic factor } F \text{ from its expected value}$$
$$= F - E[F]$$
$$\beta_{ij} = \text{sensitivity of return } R_i \text{ to factor } j$$
$$e_i = \text{random error term unique to security } i$$

In equilibrium, the equation for expected return on a security is given by:

$$E[R_i] = a_0 + b_{i1} \bar{F}_1 + b_{i2} \bar{F}_2 + \cdots + b_{in} \bar{F}_n \qquad (10.5)$$

with

$$E[R_I] = \text{expected return of security } i$$
$$a_0 = \text{expected return on zero-systematic risk security}$$
$$\text{i.e., } b_{ij} = 0 \ \forall j$$
$$F_j = \text{risk premium for factor } j$$
$$= E[F] - a_0$$

In the case of CAPM, (10.5) is:

$$E[R_i] = R_F + \beta_i [E[R_M] - R_F] \qquad (10.6)$$

where $E[R_M] - R_F$ is the market risk premium.

10.7.2   Problems with the model

1. APT factors are not well specified *ex-ante*. That is, we do not know (with certainty) what collection of factors will explain the differences in security returns.

2. The size and/or sign of F's must be estimated as well.

However, some researches have found these factors influence returns and are incorporated in prices:

1. Changes in expected inflation

2. Unanticipated changes in inflation

3. unanticipated changes in industrial production

4. unanticipated changes in default-risk premiums

5. unanticipated changes in the term structure of interest rates

6. the long-run expected growth rate of profits for the economy

7. residual market risk

10.7.3   Using APT in investment decisions

1. Forecast a factor realization

2. emphasize or deemphasize that factor

Risk-adjusted Return Measures (chapter 22 10e/11e)

11.1 Portfolio performance evaluation framework

11.1.1 Obvious factors

Risk levels Do not compare returns in isolation. Consider risk. Are returns large enough considering risk?

Time periods Ensure you are comparing performance over the same time period. Mutual fund companies with their fund performance, financial firms with their "proprietary index", and your friends tend to quote returns that cast a favorable light.

Appropriate benchmarks A 20% return is fine as long as it is better than a *suitable* benchmark index.

Investment policy Don't blame the manager, blame the policy. Consider investment policy when evaluating performance.

Past performance Past performance is no guarantee of future performance. Short-term results may be (are often) misleading.

Fees Do not forget transaction costs and expense ratios. A fund may quote a high return, but you need to check if it is *net* of management fees.

11.1.2 Available information sources

Morningsar.com Rate mutual funds from 1 to 5 stars in 48 distinct categories. Rating is based on risk-adjusted performance. Also rank fund performance over 1, 3, 5, and 10 years.

finance.yahoo.com Lots of information on mutual funds, indexes, and stocks.

11.1.3 AIMR's presentation standards

The Association for Investment Management and Research has issued (1993) *minimum* standards for presenting investment performance called the PPS (performance presentation standards).

If I knew about AIMR PPS, why did I leave the comment about fees? Ever see a "certified by AIMR" stamp on a fund's return numbers? Probably not as this (1) would open up AIMR to liability and (2) would require companies to pay for the certification. Is this a case for government intervention? Perhaps not. More a case for buyer beware. Government should require that the information on fees be provided, but perhaps not details on how it is presented.

11.2 Return and risk considerations

11.2.1 Return measures

Total return We have seen the total return formula before:

$$R_P = \frac{V_E - V_B}{V_B} = \frac{V_E}{V_B} - 1 = TR \tag{11.1}$$

multiply by 100% to get a percentage.

Dollar-weighted return Aka, Internal Rate of Return. IRR can be calculated from the following:

$$V_B = \sum_{t=1}^{N} \frac{CF_t}{(1 + IRR)^t} \tag{11.2}$$

In general, one should not use IRR to evaluate alternatives. Why? (1) Like YTM, it presumes cash flows are re-invested at IRR. (2) If fund manager A receives investments of 1M all at the beginning of the period, and manager B receives half at the beginning and half at the end, fund A will appear to have better performance. If bored, lookup MIRR on www.wikipedia.com.

Time-weighted returns TWRs are a fancy name for geometric mean of sub-period returns. This measure isolates the performance of the manager from the actions of the client (i.e., when the fund receives cash inflows).

Which measure to use? TWR, in fact, AIMR PPS require returns be computed with TWR approach.

11.2.2   Risk measures

There are two components to risk:

$$\text{total risk} = \text{systematic risk} + \text{non-systematic risk}$$
$$= \text{non-diversifiable risk} + \text{diversifiable risk}$$

Systematic risk is measured by beta and total risk is measured by standard deviation. A couple notes on beta:

1. It is only an estimate

2. It can be calculated using daily, weekly, monthly, quarterly, or annual returns. Different period returns will produce different values of beta which could impact performance rankings.

3. It is based on historical data

4. It does vary over time

11.3   Risk-adjusted performance measures

11.3.1   Sharpe Ratio

Definition. The reward-to-variability measure (RVAR, a.k.a., the Sharpe Ratio) is an *ex-post* performance measurement calculated as the ratio of excess return to standard deviation:

$$RVAR = \frac{\overline{TR}_p - \overline{R}_F}{\sigma_p} \tag{11.3}$$

where

$$\overline{TR}_p = \text{portfolio } p \text{ average TR}$$
$$\overline{R}_F = \text{average risk-free rate of return}$$
$$\sigma_p = \text{portfolio standard deviation}$$
$$\overline{TR}_p - \overline{R}_F = \text{excess return (risk premium)}$$

Portfolios, *of a given category*, can be ranked via RVAR. You want the portfolio with higher RVAR. I mention "of a given category" because a bond fund may have a superior RVAR to a mid-cap fund because of the small denominator effect. See Table 22-2 (9e), Table 22-1 (10e, 11e), Table 22-3 (9e), and Table 22-2 (10e, 11e).

Note: if you sort the data in Table 22-3 (9e) or Table 22-2 (10e, 11e) by RVAR, you will notice ranking by RVAR, RVOL, or Alpha yields the same order.

11.3.2 Treynor performance measure

Definition. Treynor's *ex-post* measure of portfolio performance, reward-to-volatility (RVOL), is calculated as the ratio of excess portfolio return to beta.

$$RVOL = \frac{\overline{TR}_p - \overline{R}_F}{\beta_p} \tag{11.4}$$

This measure was developed under the assumption that portfolios are well diversified such that non-systematic, or idiosyncratic, or firm-specific risk have been offset within the portfolio.

Sharpe vs. Treynor If portfolio is well-diversified, use the Treynor ratio. If the portfolio is not well diversified, use the Sharpe ratio. Note well diversified does not mean a beta of 1.

11.3.3 Measuring diversification

R^2, the **coefficient of determination**, is used to asses the diversification of a portfolio. In computing beta:

$$R_{it} = \alpha_i + \beta_i R_{Mt} + \epsilon_{it} \tag{11.5}$$

the regression analysis will output R^2 which measures how much of the variation in R_{it} is explained by R_{Mt}. The maximum value is 1.0. A lower value indicates factors other than overall market return, α_i and ϵ_i, explain the variation in R_{it}. These other factors represent non-market risk (could be idiosyncratic risk) that could be diversified away. In other words:

- high $R^2 \rightarrow$ more diversification

- low $R^2 \rightarrow$ less diversification

Interesting thought: apply this to the evaluation of stocks. I would argue you want the stock with the lowest R^2. Why? It *may* indicate the company is focused on its core business and not wasting time and resources diversifying what I am already diversifying in my portfolio.

Back to mutual funds: if you are holding a bunch of funds, you probably want low R^2 on all of them but high *Sharpe* ratios. If you are holding just one, you want a high R^2 (which indicates idiosyncratic risk has been eliminated from the portfolio) and a high Treynor ratio.

11.3.4 Jensen's alpha

Definition. Jensen's measure of portfolio performance calculated as the difference between what the portfolio actually earned and what it was expected to earn given its level of systematic risk.

$$\alpha_p = (\overline{R}_p - \overline{R}_F) - \beta_p(\overline{R}_M - \overline{R}_F) \tag{11.6}$$

So where does this come from? Begin with CAPM:

$$E[R_{pt}] = R_{Ft} + \beta_P(E[R_{Mt}] - R_{Ft}) \tag{11.7}$$

Note this is a model for *ex-ante* period t. By assuming investors expectations are on average fulfilled, (11.7) can be applied to *ex-post* data with the approximation:

$$R_{pt} = R_{Ft} + \beta_P(R_{Mt} - R_{Ft}) + \epsilon_{pt} \tag{11.8}$$

where

$$R_{pt} = \text{return on portfolio } p \text{ in period } t$$
$$R_{Ft} = \text{risk-free rate in period } t$$
$$R_{Mt} = \text{market return in period } t$$
$$\epsilon_{pt} = \text{random error term for portfolio } p \text{ in period } t$$
$$R_{Mt} - R_{pt} = \text{market risk premium during period } t$$

Note: the relationship between (11.8) and (11.7) is readily seen by applying the expectations operator to (11.8) and assuming $E[\epsilon_{pt}] = 0$ (the assumption that investor expectations are fulfilled on average). Rewriting (11.8):

$$R_{pt} - R_{Ft} = \beta_P(R_{Mt} - R_{Ft}) + \epsilon_{pt} \tag{11.9}$$

Notice there is no intercept term in (11.9). This is the equilibrium CAPM condition: risk premium for any asset (or portfolio) should be related to the risk premium of the market. Jensen argued that an intercept term could be added to (11.9):

$$R_{pt} - R_{Ft} = \alpha_p + \beta_P(R_{Mt} - R_{Ft}) + \epsilon_{pt} \tag{11.10}$$

Three outcomes of α_p are possible:

1. $\alpha_p = 0$ (or not statistically different from zero[1]): indicates the CAPM equilibrium condition held and the portfolio manager matched the market's risk-adjusted return

2. $\alpha_p > 0$ (and significant): portfolio manager had superior risk-adjusted performance

3. $\alpha_p < 0$ (and significant): portfolio manager had inferior risk-adjusted performance

Jensen's alpha by itself should not be used to rank portfolios. Why not? It does not incorporate risk. If you divide Jensen's alpha by beta then you will get identical rankings to the Treynor measure.

Composite measure comparison

- Well diversified portfolios $\rightarrow$ all three will agree on ranking

- Not well diversified $\rightarrow$ Treynor and Jensen measures rank undiversified portfolios higher than the Sharpe measure.

- Seems to me the most precise measure would be alpha over sigma.

---

[1]statistical significance is assessed by the t-value reported by most regression packages. For a sufficient number of observations, t-values larger than 2 (in magnitude) represent significance at the 5% level. Values less than 2 indicate the parameter is not statistically different from zero

11.4   Portfolio measurement problems

1. Based on CAPM and its assumptions. For instance, using the T-bill as the risk-free rate and assuming borrowing and lending at the same rate.

2. The choice of market portfolio is debatable: we already talked about shortcomings of the S&P 500. Only VWRET and EWRET from CRSP are true market portfolios.

3. Choice of market portfolio does not include the entire investment universe (i.e.[2], world markets)

11.5   Other issues in performance evaluation

Monitoring   Run the numbers more than once

Performance attribution   Is it from market timing (trend following), security selection (fundamental analysis), or luck? See footnote 12 on page 603 for ways to decompose performance.

Can performance be predicted   No. Most studies suggest a weak correlation between past relative performance and future relative performance (be it positive or negative).

---

[2]i.e. = id est, e.g. = exempli gratia

TWELVE

Common Stock Valuation (chapter 10 10e/11e)

12.1 Key concepts

1. Understand foundation for valuation of common stocks, discounted cash-flow techniques, and the concept of intrinsic value

2. use the dividend model to estimate the prices of stocks

3. understand the P/E ratio as well as the determinants of the P/E ratio

4. Analyze stocks on the basis of relative valuation techniques

12.2 Discounted cash flow techniques

The estimated value for any security is given by:

$$V_0 = \sum_{i=1}^{n} \frac{CF_t}{(1+k)^t} \qquad (12.1)$$

where $k =$ the appropriate discount rate (or required rate of return). To estimate such a model:

1. estimate the appropriate k

2. estimate the amount and timing of future cash flow streams

3. compare V_0 with current market price

12.2.1   The required rate of return

The required rate of return, k, is the minimum $E[R]$ necessary to induce an investor to buy, given the associated risk. One way to estimate is to utilize CAPM to compute the required rate of return.

12.2.2   expected cash flows

Several questions need to be answered when estimating expected cash flows:

1. what are the cash flows to use in valuing a stock?

2. what are the expected amounts of the cash flows?

3. when will the expected cash flows be received

Since dividends are the only cash flow stream investors receive under normal conditions, it is useful to consider the dividend discount model (DDM). Earnings (EPS) are not paid directly to investors but are useful for measures for other means of valuation (e.g., P/E ratio).

12.2.3   The dividend discount model

The DDM is a model for determining the estimated price of a stock by discounting all future dividends.

   Replace CF with D to get the dividend discount model. Point out that at infinity, the value of dividends are worth very little today. We must also consider several dividend growth rate cases (zero growth rate, constant growth rate, multiple growth rate)

12.2.3.1   Zero growth model

Given a constant dividend expected for *all future time periods* and required rate of return k, the present value of such a security is:

$$V_0 = \frac{D_0}{k} \qquad (12.2)$$

12.2.3.2 Constant growth rate model

If dividends are expected to grow at a constant rate g, then the present value of a security is:

$$V_0 = \frac{D_1}{k - g} \qquad (12.3)$$

Note: D_1 and not D_0. The value today depends on next period's dividend. This *model* is used quite often because it has been the best estimate of expected dividend streams for a "lot" of companies and the market as a whole. Think of g as inflation plus something else.

Example 1 YourCorp is currently paying $1/share. Investors expect dividends to grow 7%/year for the foreseeable future. Given YourCorp's risk, $k = 15\%$. What is V_0?

The constant growth model implies that dividends, earnings, and stock prices are all expected to grow at the rate g. To see this, let $t = 1$ and re-do Example 1.

As you can see from (12.3), two factors significantly impact a firm's stock price:

1. The market's required rate of return k

2. Expectation of dividend growth rate g

However, investors may have different k's and expectations of g (note: this is unlike the homogeneous expectations assumption of CAPM). Therefore some investors will be willing to sell, some willing to buy (i.e., liquidity in markets is due to heterogeneous expectations).

12.2.3.3 Multiple growth rate

In the MGRM, there are multiple growth rates (how intuitive?). How many? As many as you like. We'll look at the common two-step model:

$$P_0 = \sum_{t=1}^{n} \frac{D_0(1 + g_s)^t}{(1 + k)^t} + \frac{D_n(1 + g_c)}{k - g_c} \frac{1}{(1 + k)^n} \qquad (12.4)$$

where

$$g_s = \text{short term super- or sub-normal dividend growth rate}$$
$$g_c = \text{long-term constant dividend growth rate}$$
$$D_n = \text{dividend at the end of the abnormal growth period}$$

Example 2 $D_0 = \$1.00$, $g_s = 12\%$, $n = 5$ years, $g_c = 6\%$, $k = 10\%$. What is P_0?

12.2.3.4   What about capital gains?

At first glance, the DDM seems to be missing capital gains. This is not true. You can compute the FV of a stock using DDM. From this FV, you will know what your capital gains are (expected to be).

12.2.3.5   Intrinsic value

The value obtained by a DDM estimation is the *intrinsic value* (V_0). If $V_0 > P_0$ then buy/hold. If $V_0 < P_0$ then avoid/sell. If $V_0 = P_0$ then stock is correctly valued.

12.2.3.6   DDM in practice

Equation (12.3) can be rearranged to calculate the required rate of return k:

$$k = \frac{D_1}{P_0} + g \qquad (12.5)$$

Now what? Could compare to the k ($E[R]$) using CAPM.

12.2.3.7   Another DDM approach: DCF

Discount cash flow approach is as follows:

1. Forecast expected *free cash flow* (FCF). FCF is cash amounts available to be paid to both debt-holders and stockholders.

2. Estimate the discount rate (required rate of return): CAPM or DDM

3. Calculate value of corporation (P_0) using (12.4) with $n = 10$.

4. Calculate intrinsic value

$$V_0 = \frac{P_0 - \text{market value of shareholder claims}}{\text{shares outstanding}} \qquad (12.6)$$

See page 273-274 and/or www.valupro.net for more information

12.3 Relative valuation techniques

By comparing measures such as P/E with other firms you avoid estimating g and k. The book mentions a "relationship" between interest rates and guess what... the S&P 500. Take a look at Table 10-1. This data is used to estimate $E[R_M]$.

an illustration...

12.3.1 Valuation using P/E ratio

Analysts and investment advisory services compute the forward P/E ratio then make an under- or over-valued judgement based on firm prospects.

Using P/E to estimate a target

1. Assume earnings grow at a constant g, therefore, $E_1 = E_0(1 + g)$ or take the average analysts' estimate of E_1

2. Use an "appropriate" P/E ratio to obtain the target price:

$$P_1 = E_1(P/E)$$

12.3.2 Price to book value

Book value measures actual values of tangible assets. However, intellectual property, which could be a source of significant future income, is not included. There is some empirical evidence that stocks with low price to book values significantly outperform the average stock.

12.3.3 Price to sales ratio

Used when companies have erratic or no earnings (i.e., hard to calculate P/E). According to the "What works on wall street" book, this is the "king" of valuation ratios. Q: Why do you think this might be the case?

12.3.4   Economic value added

EVA = operating profit - company's cost of capital

12.4   Final thoughts

"Stocks are worth what investors pay for them"

THIRTEEN

Bond Valuation (chapter 17 10e/11e)

13.1 Key concepts

1. Understand and calculate various bond yield measures

2. Calculate bond prices

3. Bond price changes

4. Bond duration

13.2 Bond yields

Interest rate Price paid by a borrower to a lender for use of resources over some time period.

Basis point 100 basis points = 1%

Short term riskless rate The "basis" for all other rates. typically the treasury *bill* rate and designated as R_F. All other rates differ in (i) maturity and (ii) risk premium.

13.2.1 Basic interest rate components

Real risk free rate (RR) The rate that must be offered to individuals to persuade saving over consumption

Nominal interest rate RR plus an adjustment for expected inflation. An *approximation* of the nominal interest rate is the *Fisher hypothesis*:

$$R_F \approx RR + EI$$

13.2.2 Measuring bond yields

The following measures are based on:

- AAA rated corporate bond

- 10% annual coupon rate

- 3 years until maturity

- semi-annual coupon payments

- face value of $1,000

- current price of $1,052.42 Q: why is this greater than $1,000?

Current yield Ratio of bond's annual coupon divided by current market price:

$$CY = \frac{\text{annual coupon}}{\text{current market price}} = \frac{10\% \times \$1,000}{\$1,052.42} = 9.5\%$$

This is better than quoting just the coupon rate because you will have to incur a cost to receive the coupon. However, does not include PV of future redemption at par value.

Yield to maturity The compound rate of return on a bond purchased at the current market price if:

1. the bond is held to maturity

2. coupons received while the bond is held are reinvested at the calculated yield to maturity

3. the bond issuer does not default

4. the bond is not callable

This rate of return, YTM, can be calculated from the following expression:

$$P = \sum_{t=1}^{n} \frac{c_t}{(1+YTM)^t} + \frac{FV}{(1+YTM)^n} \tag{13.1}$$

where

$P =$ current price of bond

$n =$ number of *semiannual* periods to maturity

$YTM =$ semiannual yield to maturity

$c_t =$ coupon payment in dollars at time t. Typically constant

$FV =$ face/maturity/par value. typically \$1,000

Substituting the values from our ongoing example: (EXAMPLE 17=2 in the book)

$$1052.42 = \sum_{t=1}^{6} \frac{50}{(1+YTM)^t} + \frac{1000}{(1+YTM)^6}$$

Using a *real* calculator: $YTM = 0.04$

Bond-equivalent yield Yield to maturity on an annual basis computed by doubling the semiannual yield to maturity.

Interesting observation There are two ways to determine if a bond is selling at a premium (discount):

1. If the market price is higher (lower) than the face value

2. If the coupon rate is higher (lower) than the *current yield*

Yield to call Corporate bonds may be callable, typically after some deferred call period. The **yield to call** measure can be extracted from:

$$P = \sum_{t=1}^{fc} \frac{c_t}{(1+YC)^t} + \frac{CP}{(1+YC)^{fc}}$$

where

$$P = \text{current price of bond}$$
$$fc = \text{number of } semiannual \text{ periods until } first \text{ call date}$$
$$YC = \text{semiannual yield to call}$$
$$c_t = \text{coupon payment in dollars at time } t. \text{ Typically constant}$$
$$CP = \text{call price to be paid by issuer}$$

Realized compound yield   One of the assumptions in the YTM calculation was reinvestment of coupon payments at the YTM rate. One can see how this assumption does not necessarily hold true. An after-the-fact measure, called *realized compound yield* can be calculated to asses the actual yield realized:

$$RCY = \left(\frac{\text{total ending wealth}}{\text{purchase price of bond}} \right)^{1/n} - 1.0$$

Reinvestment risk   Again, YTM assumes coupon payments (interest payments) are reinvested at the YTM rate and gain interest again. See example 17-5 for an example of **interest on interest**. Since interest rates are not constant, one can not reasonably expect *all* future reinvestment of coupon payments to be at the YTM.

Reinvestment rate risk   The risk that future reinvestment rates will be less than the YTM at the time bond was purchased. See Table 17-1 (10e, 11e) for an illustration of the impact of varied reinvestment rates and note the large percentage of total *dollar* return attributable to reinvestment.

Horizon return   So current yield does not incorporate return of principle and YTM assumes a constant reinvestment rate equal to the YTM. The **horizon (total) return** is an estimate of total return based on explicit reinvestment rate assumptions. DISSERTATION IDEA: would be interesting to model horizon return using stochastic interest rate modeling.

13.3   Bond prices

Value of any financial asset = present value of all future cash flows discounted at rate appropriate for asset. For bonds, we've seen the equation before:

$$P = \sum_{t=1}^{n} \frac{c_t}{(1+r)^t} + \frac{FV}{(1+r)^n} \tag{13.2}$$

where r is the appropriate semiannual discount rate or market yield. Note:

Table 13.1: Discount rate interpretations

Rate	Meaning
$r < coupon$	bond will sell at a *premium*
$r = coupon$	bond will sell at *par value*
$r > coupon$	bond will sell at a *discount*

13.4   Bond price changes

13.4.1   Changes over time

Ultimately, bonds will be worth their face value as the maturity date approaches. Before the maturity date however, interest rates and bond prices do change.

13.4.2   Malkiel theorems

Burton Malkiel (1962) derived five bond price and yield theorems. Here we present three. See Table 17-2 (10e, 11e) to help understand the following theorems and corollaries.

Theorem 1. *Bond price-interest rate relationship: Bond prices move inversely to interest rates. This is evident by equation (13.1). In equation form:*

$$\frac{\partial P}{\partial r} < 0$$

where r is the market yield (or YTM).

Proof. Simply take the partial derivative with respect to r of (13.2):

$$\frac{\partial P}{\partial r} = \sum_{t=1}^{n} \frac{-c_t t(1+r)^{t-1}}{((1+r)^t)^2} + \frac{-FVn(1+r)^{n-1}}{((1+r)^n)^2}$$

$$= -\left(\sum_{t=1}^{n} c_t t(1+r)^{-t-1} + FVn(1+r)^{-n-1} \right) < 0$$

$\square$

Corollary. *Percentage change - interest rate relationship*[1]*: A decrease in rates will raise bond prices more on a percentage basis than a corresponding increase in rates will lower prices.*

Proof. Simplify the bond price equation to be $P = 1/X$ where X embodies the interest rate. The *percent change* in bond price for an *increase* in interest rates is:

$$\frac{P_1}{P_0} = \frac{\frac{1}{X+z}}{\frac{1}{X}} = \frac{X}{X+z}$$

Similarly the *percent change* in bond price for a corresponding decrease *decrease* is:

$$\frac{P_1}{P_0} = \frac{\frac{1}{X-z}}{\frac{1}{X}} = \frac{X}{X-z}$$

Clearly the percent change for a decrease is larger than the percent change for an increase:

$$\frac{X}{X-z} > \frac{X}{X+z}$$

$\square$

Theorem 2. *Bond price - maturity relationship: As interest rates change, the prices of longer term bonds will change more than the prices of shorter term bonds,* ceratis paribus. *Let ΔP_n and ΔP_m represent the the change in prices for bonds with maturities n and m, respectively. Furthermore let $n > m$. In equation form:*

$$\frac{\partial \Delta P_n}{\partial r} > \frac{\partial \Delta P_m}{\partial r}$$

---

[1]Corollary: a proposition that follows from one already proven

Proof. Clearly the longer the maturity, the more terms that are added in (13.2). □

Example. Consider two bonds:

	Bond N	Bond M
Coupon	10%	10%
Maturity	15 yr	30 yr
Price @ $YTM = 12\%$	862	838
Price @ $YTM = 10\%$	1000	1000
Price @ $YTM = 8\%$	1173	1226

As shown, in either case (increase from 10 to 12 or decrease from 10 to 8), the change in bond price is larger for the longer maturity bond M.

Corollary. *Percentage change - maturity relationship: As TTM increases, the percentage price change that occurs increases at a diminishing rate. Let* $\%\Delta P$ *represent the percentage price change that occurs from a change in interest rate. Restating Theorem 2 in equation form:*

$$\frac{\partial(\%\Delta P)}{\partial TTM} > 0$$

This Corollary states:

$$\frac{\partial^2(\%\Delta P)}{\partial TTM^2} < 0$$

Proof. Maybe next semester. □

Theorem 3. *Bond - coupon price relationship: Bond price* volatility, *measured in terms of percentage-price fluctuations, is inversely related to* coupon rate *(not the YTM). Let* $\%\Delta P$ *represent the bond price percentage change as a result of a change in interest rates. In equation form:*

$$\frac{\partial(\%\Delta P)}{\partial c} < 0$$

Proof. Given two bonds, X and Y, identical in all aspects sans coupon rate. The prices of each bonds at different YTMs are shown below: □

	Bond X	Bond Y
Coupon	10% (100)	15% (150)
Maturity	15 yr	15 yr
Price @ $YTM = 10\%$	1000	1384
Price @ $YTM = 15\%$	705	1000
$\%\Delta P$	29.5%	27.7%

As shown, the percentage change in bond price *decreases* as the coupon rate *increases*, the inverse relationship we were looking for.

13.4.3   Malkiel theorem implications

1. If interest rates are anticipated to *decline* → purchase low-coupon, long-maturity bonds

2. If interest rates are anticipated to *rise* → purchase short-maturity, high-coupon bonds.

Table 13.2: Malkiel Theorem Implications

	r increase	r decrease
$\frac{\partial P}{\partial r} < 0$ (The 1)	decrease	increase
$\frac{\partial (\%\Delta P)}{\partial TTM} > 0$ (The 2)	want *short* maturity to *minimize* exposure to price *decrease*	want *long* maturity to *maximize* exposure to price *increase*
$\frac{\partial (\%\Delta P)}{\partial c} < 0$ (The 3)	want *high* coupons to *minimize* exposure to bond price *decrease*	want *low* coupons to *maximize* exposure to price *increase*

13.4.4   Duration

13.4.4.1   Definition / calculation

TTM: Time until you receive face value

Duration: time weighted average of all payments (face value *and* coupon) received

Duration is a measure of a bond's lifetime that accounts for the entire pattern of cash flows over the life of the bond. In other words, the weighted average of payment receipt times. Duration is calculated by:

$$D = \sum_{i=1}^{n} \frac{PV[CF_t]}{P} \times t$$

$$= \sum_{i=1}^{n} \frac{1}{P} \frac{CF_t}{(1+YTM)^t} \times t \tag{13.3}$$

Note:

1. this is considered a *weighted average* because the present value of *all* cash flows discounted at YTM *is* P

2. CF_t includes *coupon* and repayment of *face value*

13.4.4.2 Interpretation

See Figure 17-4 (10e) or Figure 18-1 (11e) for a graphical depiction of the subtle difference between *maturity* and *duration*:

This figure illustrates the subtle difference:

- Maturity - when you will receive repayment of principal (or face value)

- Duration - weighted average of when you will receive *all* payments

Relationships between duration and TTM, YTM, and coupon rate are as follows:

1. Duration increases with time to maturity but at a decreasing rate:

$$\frac{\partial D}{\partial TTM} > 0, \quad \frac{\partial^2 D}{\partial TTM^2} < 0$$

2. Duration is inversely related to YTM, *ceratis paribus*.

$$\frac{\partial D}{\partial YTM} < 0$$

   Pretty easy to see, YTM is in the denominator of (13.3)

3. Duration is inversely related to coupon size (rate).

$$\frac{\partial D}{\partial C} < 0$$

   A little more difficult but can be shown by substituting (13.1) into (13.3).

Why is duration important?

1. A more precise measure of interest rate sensitivity

2. Used in certain bond-management strategies such as immunization

13.4.4.3   Estimating price changes using duration

A measure called **modified duration** can be used to *estimate* interest rate sensitivity.

$$D^* = \frac{D}{1 + YTM} \tag{13.4}$$

From this expression, the percentage change in bond price, $\Delta P/P$ can be estimated as follows:

$$\Delta P/P \approx -D^* \times \Delta YTM \tag{13.5}$$

13.4.4.4   Convexity

For small changes in YTM, equation (13.5) provides a good approximation. However, as changes in YTM increase, the accuracy is diminished. See Figure 17-3 (10e) or Figure 18-2 (11e). Therefore you can simply revert back to equation (13.1) for precise calculations.

13.4.4.5   Some conclusions

1. If you anticipate interest rate decline → you want long duration bonds with high convexity to maximize the price increase

2. If you anticipate interest rate rises → you want short duration bonds with high convexity to minimize the price decline

Recall from Table 13.2: if rates *increase*, we want *short* maturity bonds (price will go down less), if rates *decrease*, we want long we want *long* maturity bonds (price will go up more).

Duration incorporates *both* maturity and coupon payments. So you can simplify your decision process by looking at just duration in anticipation of rate increases or decreases.

Part III

Fundamental Analysis

FOURTEEN

Market Efficiency (chapter 12 10e/11e)

14.1 Key concepts

1. Understand and analyze the efficient market hypothesis ("EMH")

2. Identify weak, semi-strong, and strong form efficiency

3. EMH tests and evidence

4. Anomalies

14.2 Concept of efficient markets

14.2.1 What is an efficient market?

Efficient Market market in which prices of securities *quickly* and *fully* reflect all known and available information. All known information includes (i) past information, (ii) current information, (iii) announced and forthcoming events, and (iv) information that can be *reasonably* inferred (e.g., Fed will raise rates next week).

14.2.2 Why we expect U.S. markets to be efficient

1. A large number of rational, profit-maximizing investors actively participate in the market by (i) analyzing, (ii) valuing, and (iii) trading stocks. One participant alone cannot affect security prices.

2. Information is costless and widely available to everyone.

3. Announcements are generated randomly (independent of one another). This one will come up later in the discussion.

4. Investors react quickly and fully to new information (about 7 minutes in the U.S.)

14.2.3   International perspective

There are greater inefficiencies in emerging markets than U.S. or developed country markets (see the list above). Therefore fund managers can take advantaged of mispriced securities. For instance, during the 1990s, 10% outperformed the S&P 500, 31% outperformed an European index, and 51% outperformed emerging markets index. Note: you'll have to be quick. Studies have shown price adjustments within one day in Europe and Asia.

14.2.4   Forms of market efficiency

Weak form efficiency Prices reflect all past price and volume information. Any patterns are already incorporated into price.

Semi-strong form efficiency Weak form + all publicly known data such as earnings, dividends, new product developments, accounting changes, fed polices, etc.

Strong form efficiency semi-strong + private information

14.3   Evidence on market efficiency

The key to testing efficiency is the *consistency* with which investors can earn *abnormal returns* - returns commensurate with (i) risk involved, (ii) information involved, and (iii) transaction costs. Related to (iii) Copeland and Copeland found a spread of up to 11.5 basis points that could be earned given U.S. - Hong Kong lag. However, the presence of transaction costs *likely* eliminate the economic possibility of arbitrage.

14.3.1   Weak form evidence

Statistical tests of price changes   Weak form efficiency implies stocks follow a random walk (recall information is assumed to arrive randomly). this can be tested with a serial correlation test or runs test.

Fama studied daily returns on 30 DJI stocks in 1965 and found a very small but positive serial correlation. Several tests by others have reached the same conclusion. Similar support of independence are also found with "runs" tests.

Note: There is still some small positive serial correlation which implies weak-form *inefficiency*. However, transaction costs will likely eliminate any potential profits.

Technical trading rules   Little evidence exists that a technical trading rule based *solely* on past price and volume data can outperform and buy-and-hold strategy

Overreaction hypothesis   Studies in 1985 and 1992 found some overreaction. Could buy a portfolio of 35 extreme losers, hold for three years, and outperform the market.

14.3.2   Semi-strong form evidence

Semi-strong efficiency is evaluated using tests of the speed of price adjustment to publicly available information. This is often accomplished with an *event study* - an empirical analysis of stock price behavior surrounding a particular event. The event study methodology is as follows:

1. begin with index model of stock returns (such as CAPM)

2. Identify company-unique returns as the residual error terms and compute the abnormal return

$$\text{abnormal return} = AR_{it} = R_{it} - E[R_{it}]$$

3. compute the cumulative abnormal return (sum of individual abnormal returns of the period of time under examination)

$$CAR_i = \sum_{t=1}^{n} AR_{it}$$

Stock splits   Fama, Fisher, Jensen, and Roll (1969) found abnormal returns prior to stock splits but normal returns post-split. Byun and Rozeff reexamined the issue in 2003 by looking at 12,747 stock splits from 1927 to 1996 and found no statistically significant abnormal returns.

Dividend announcements   Studies generally agree that the market adjusts rapidly to new information.

IPOs   You can get abnormal profits if one of the fortunate few able to purchase at the offering price (since underwriters typically underprice). However, the market does adjust *very quickly* to true values. See footnote 15 on page 323.

Reactions to economic news   One study found no price impacts that lasted beyond the announcement day. Even a study of hourly stock price data showed reactions to surprise announcements were impounded in prices within one hour. Published rumors do not lead to significant abnormal returns. However, a cumulative excess return of approximately 7% occurs in the calendar month prior to rumor publication.

14.3.3   Strong form evidence

One way to test to examine if "VPs" can consistently earn above average risk-adjusted returns. Also, can an investor use the value of the information in a superior manner?

Corporate insiders   Evidence shows corporate insiders do earn abnormal profits on their trades. This is indeed a violation of strong form efficiency. Other studies show the *magnitude* of abnormal returns are low.

14.4   Implications of the EMH

For technical analysis   Evidence supports EMH. Burden of proof lies on technical analysis proponents, and they must include transaction costs, risks, taxes, time commitment, and any other factors to make a fair comparison).

For fundamental analysis   No theoretical reason why an investor could *not* do a superior job of analysis and profit thereby. However, there are lots of people (and supercomputers) out there looking at the same data and making the same interpretations.

For money management   First the evidence. From 1982 (start of bull market) through 1998 the Vanguard 500 Index fund had an annual average return of 19.7%. The average large-cap fund averaged 18.2%, and the average equity fund averaged 15.9%. Also, from 1993 to 2002, the same index fund outperformed almost 75% of all U.S. diversified stock funds (not including funds that disappeared during the period)[1].

---

[1]Note that it is virtually impossible to consistently identify, in advance, the 25% of actively managed stock funds that *did* do better than the index funds.

So presuming the market is "economically efficient" what is left for the money manager to do?

1. Diversification

2. Portfolio risk

3. Be mindful of taxes

4. Economize on transaction costs

For individual investors Do you have the time?

14.5 Evidence of market anomalies

Market anomalies Techniques or strategies that appear to be contrary to an efficient market.

Several anomalies exist:

1. Unexpected earnings - market appears to adjust with a lag to earnings surprises

2. Low P/E ratios - low P/E ratio stocks outperform high P/E stocks

3. Size effect - Observed tendency for smaller firms to have higher stock returns than large firms

4. The January effect - Observed tendency for small-cap stocks to have higher returns in January than in other months. Possibly due to tax-induced sales in December (prompting a decrease in prices) which then recover in January

5. Value Line's performance - The Value Line rankings for timeliness have performed extremely well from 1965 to 2002 and appear to offer the average investor a chance to outperform the averages.

FIFTEEN

Economy Analysis (chapter 13 10e/11e)

15.1 Key concepts

Hindsight is 20/20

1. Stock market / economy relationship

2. Conceptual determinants of the stock market

3. Basic market level forecasts

This chapter is focused on understanding the *direction* of markets in the near to mid-term (1 to 5 years). Not a major consideration for those who follow a buy-and-hold strategy.

15.2 Global perspective

Don't ignore the rest of the world. What applies here applies there.

15.3 Assessing the economy

Gross domestic product The market value of final goods and services produced by an economy over some time period

- Gross domestic product ("GDP") is a measure of "the economy".

- Naturally GDP varies over time and impacts businesses which in turns impacts stock market performance.

- These ups and downs are referred to as the *business cycle.*

15.3.1   The business cycle

Business cycle The recurring patterns of expansion and contraction in an economy.

- Expansions average about 29 months, contractions less than 12

- These are only averages, the standard deviation is high (think expansion from 3/1991 to 3/2001)

- Several composite economic indexes are used to asses the economy

    - Leading: stock prices, index of consumer expectations, money supply, interest rate spread (yield curve?)
    - Coincident: industrial production, manufacturing sales, trade sales
    - Lagging: Duration of unemployment, commercial and industrial loans outstanding

Note how Example 13-1 shows *NBER* Identified recession began 6 months after it actually began, and declared it ended 1.5 years after it actually ended.

Global perspective   Other countries experienced the downturn with us. An ode to global integration.

Has the business cycle been tamed?   In other words, is the cyclical nature gone? No. The 10th recession on record began in March 2001. Will we have another bubble? Who knows?

Stock market and the business cycle   Recall stock prices are part of the *leading* composite economic indexes. Evidence shows it does lead (e.g., stock prices turn up 3 to 5 months prior to a recovery), albeit imperfectly.

15.3.2 Bond market, stock market, economy

- Yield curves are useful in forecasting the economy.

- Think back to CAPM and the role of R_F

15.3.3 Forecasts of the economy

- In contrast to financial analysts forecasts, macroeconomic forecast accuracy *appears* to have increased over time

- The money supply is connected to economic activity: increase in supply $\rightarrow$ increase in activity; increase in demand $\rightarrow$ reduction in economic activity. Why? (think interest rates)

- no real conclusions on optimal monetary policy (the classical "invisible hand" vs. Keynesian required government intervention fight)

- The yield curve shape *is* related to the current business cycle stage

  - early expansion stages: yield curve *tends* to be low and upward sloping
  - approaching peak of cycle: yield curve *tends* to be high and downward sloping. Note *every* recession since WWII has been preceded by a downward sloping yield curve. See Figure 13-2 (10e, 11e) of the text or Figure 19.1 on page 86.

- Consensus forecasts are also available

15.4 Understanding the stock market

- Q: What is "the market?"

- What determines aggregate stock prices?

  - Interest rates, expected interest rates $\rightarrow$ think R_f in CAPM
  - expected earnings $\rightarrow$ think NPV of all future cash flows

- If I may do a bit of self-promotion: bring up VWPE document

15.5   Making market forecasts

An example...

Industry Analysis (chapter 14 10e/11e)

16.1   Key concepts

1. Sector/industry analysis in top-down approach context: aggregate market and economic indicators are favorable for investment, step two is industry analysis

2. Industry classification

3. Investors' use of industry analysis

16.2   Classifying industries

Standard Industrial Classification A classification of firms on the basis of what they *produce* using census data.

Global Industry Classification Standard Provides a complete continuous set of global sector and industry definitions using 10 economic sectors SIC is the most commonly used system[1]

NAICS is also popular. Fama and French also have developed industry classifications based on 5-49 industries.

---

[1]http://www.osha.gov/pls/imis/sic_manual.html

16.3   Importance of industry/sector analysis

Long run Industries are cyclical and perform differently over the long run. See Table 14-1 (10e, 11e) for the long-run performance of a few industries.

Short run Telecom is a good example of an industry moving in and out of favor. See Figure 14-1 (9e, 11e). .

Cross-sectional volatility The variation in returns across sectors of the market has risen. Quoting the August 2002 Money magazine article (which you can find on the web): "In general, the higher the level of cross-sector volatility in a given month, the wider the gap in returns between leading and lagging sectors" Accurate forecasts with appropriate long and short positions could prove very profitable.

16.4   Industry life cycle

Industry life cycle The stages of an industry's evolution from pioneering to stabilization and decline.

The four stages:

Pioneering Rapid growth in demand, highly competitive, high risk, high expected returns

Expansion Surviving pioneers are identifiable, the continue to grow but at a slower rate. Could see product improvements and price declines.

Stabilization Growth begins to moderate, perhaps the longest stage of the industry life cycle. Important for management improve operating efficiency.

Declining stage home radios, black-and-white televisions... more generally, think substitute products like solid-state memory versus magnetic cores or vacuum tubes.

What stage is the industry under consideration in? Risk tolerance + understanding of life cycle stage = appropriate investment.

16.4.1   Qualitative industry analysis

Competition   Porter's five forces model is a tool for industry analysis. See Figure 14-2 (10e) or Figure 14-3 (11e).

Government effects   Breakup of AT&T, coagulation.

Structural changes   Industrial $\rightarrow$ information and technology $\rightarrow$ services? Qualitative analysis: How will industry under consideration be impacted by the five forces in the near term?

16.5   Using sector/industry analysis as an investor

Consider the business cycle and the impact on broad industry classifications: growth industries, defensive industries, cyclical industries, and interest-sensitive industries.

16.5.1   Picking industries for next year

Read Box 14-1.

SEVENTEEN

Company Analysis (chapter 15 10e/11e)

17.1 Key concepts

- Analyze companies using fundamental analysis

  1. Return on equity (ROE)
  2. Return on assets (ROA)
  3. Price to earnings (PE)

- Understand accounting issues and controversies

- Importance of earnings announcements and surprises

17.2 Fundamental analysis

Short-run intrinsic value can be estimated as follows:

$$V_0 = \text{estimated EPS} \times \text{expected P/E ratio}$$
$$= E[E_1] \times E[P/E]$$

Q: Why focus on earnings?

17.3 Accounting aspects of earnings

Okay, so earnings are important, just what are they?

17.3.1   Financial statements

Q: What are the three major financial statements?

Balance sheet   assets = liabilities + shareholder's equity. See Exhibit 15-1 on page 398 for a sample balance sheet. Several ratios can be calculated from this balance sheet:

1. Leverage = debt/total assets. This can be a measure for risk. More risk → expected more return

2. current ratio = current assets divided by current liabilities. This measures ability to meet short-term debt obligations. A ratio between 1 and 1.5 is considered standard.

3. and others ...

Income statement   See Exhibit 15-2 on page 400 for a sample income statement. Measures current management performance and company profitability. The key item is after-tax net income which is used to calculate EPS:

$$EPS = \frac{\text{after tax net income}}{\text{number of common shares outstanding}} \qquad (17.1)$$

However, we often see earnings "explanations" that disentangle extraordinary items (e.g., acquisitions, Katrina, etc.) from continuing operations. Also, note the impact of accounting changes on net income and net income per share. Don't forget taxes.

Cash-flow statement   See Exhibit 15-3 on page 402 for a sample Cash-flow statement. Tracks the flow of cash through the firm and consists of three parts:

1. cash from *operating* activities - net income (money in); foreign currency adjustments (money in or out)

2. cash from *investing* activities - purchase of PPE (money out) sale of investments or other assets (money in)

3. cash from *financing* activities - issue debt (money in) issue dividends (money out)

Items to look for in financial statements:

1. net cash used for inventories - a lot of money spent on inventories means stuff is not being sold, wrong products are being made, market is bad, etc. Q: Which statement?

2. "write-offs" - allegedly one-time charges but some firms overuse these. e.g., "reorganization charge" or "charge for acquisition." Q: Which statement?

3. accounts receivables increases - trouble collecting money (chose the wrong customers?) Q: Which statement?

4. accounts payable rising - trouble paying the bills Q: Which statement?

Certifying the statements GAAP - financial reporting requirements establishing the rules for producing financial statements. Adherence is certified by an auditor (Arthur Anderson, Enron).

Do not ignore the footnotes This is important. Very important information is typically buried in footnotes:

1. accounting methods used

2. any ongoing litigation -e.g., Blackberry and NTP

3. how revenue is recognized

Do not ignore them.

17.3.2 Problems with EPS

Reported earnings Are "reported" earnings the *true* earnings? Earnings management can occur via "loopholes" or areas of subjective judgement in GAAP. E.g., "discretionary accruals", when revenue is recognized, off-balance sheet activities (Enron), firm's use of hedging, etc. Regarding hedging, the FAS133[1] standard and supporting documents total 800 pages. Q: What does this mean?

---

[1] Accounting for Derivative Instruments and Hedging Activities

Quality of earnings Due to the subjectivity and potential for manipulation in reported earnings, one must consider the quality of earnings. A couple ways to combat the problem:

1. Use your expertise in accounting and financial analysis to determine earnings for yourself

2. Us the first item on the income statement (sales or revenues) - although they can be manipulated also, at least you catch the number before additional manipulation opportunities arise as you drill down to earnings.

Pro Forma earnings To add to the confusion, companies also report "pro-forma" earnings. Three types of reported earnings:

- Net income - the official audited "reported" earnings

- Pro Forma earnings - un-audited earnings that leaves out costs said to be irrelevant to ongoing business that can be calculated however you like

- EBITDA aka operating profit - revenue less operating expenses but leaves out expenses. Sometime used to mask the lack of real profitability. Good example is 2001 Quest communications: EBITDA was $1.77 but actually loss was $142 million due to negation of operating profit by interest and depreciation expenses. In 2002, stock dropped almost 90%.

What investors can do Some of this we mentioned earlier:

- Examine filings for additional information - pay attention to footnotes

- Obtain other opinions - e.g., Value Line Investment Survey. An aside, if I were really interested in the analysis of firms, I would see if firms like Value Line are hiring for internships or full-time post-graduation.

- Use *Free Cash Flow* which is cash flow from operations less capital expenditures and dividends. It is more difficult to disguise cash-flow problems. Firms need cash to operate.

17.3.3 International accounting

Accounting standards vary but some convergence is observed. Keep differences in mind when evaluating foreign companies' financial statements. For example, comparing leverage across borders may yield deviations from the truth as to which firm has more bankruptcy risk.

17.4 Analyzing a company's profitability

Several ratios to consider:

$$EPS = \frac{\text{net income after taxes}}{\text{shares outstanding}}$$

$$ROE = \frac{\text{net income after taxes}}{\text{stockholders' equity}}$$

$$ROA = \frac{\text{net income after taxes}}{\text{total assets}}$$

$$\text{book value per share} = \frac{\text{stockholders' equity}}{\text{shares outstanding}}$$

$$\text{leverage} = \frac{\text{total liabilities}}{\text{stockholders' equity}}$$

$$\text{profit margin} = \frac{\text{net income [after taxes]}}{\text{sales}}$$

$$\text{turnover} = \frac{\text{sales}}{\text{total assets}}$$

From accounting data one can measure the *sustainable growth rate*, g, which represents the rate at which a company can grow without the issuance of additional securities. To compute g, begin with the the dividend payout ratio (DPR):

$$DPR = \frac{\text{dividend per share}}{\text{earnings per share}}$$

Q: Where do we get dividend per share from? Then calculate the retention rate as:

$$\text{retention rate} = 1 - DPR$$

Then arrive at the internal growth rate:

$$g = ROE \times (1 - DPR) = ROE \times \text{retention rate}$$

Problems with such a measure:

1. Forecast based on one year of data

2. May be better to use average of historical data

3. *ROE* varies over time as well and may be better to estimate

17.5   Obtaining earnings estimates

Calculations thus far have been based on historical earnings measures (once it is in the annual report, it is history). In contrast, the EPS used to value stocks is the expected earnings. When using earnings *estimates* three things must be considered: estimate accuracy, impact of earnings surprises, and the earnings game.

There are essentially two sources of earnings estimates:

1. Security analysts: Evidence shows no particular analyst is better than another therefore consensus forecast should be used.

2. Do it yourself: with various modeling techniques based on available data (typically historical time series data). As usual, results are mixed. May be done by the analysts already.

17.5.1   Estimate accuracy

Guess what? Analyst estimates are typically wrong in practice (average annual error of 44 percent). If you can do better than analysts with your statistical models then you can expect to "profit from your astuteness".

17.5.2   impact of earnings surprises

What happens when estimate is proven wrong? We have a model developed by Latane and Jones (1977) to compute **standardized unexpected earnings** (SUE):

$$SUE = \frac{\text{actual quarterly EPS - forecast quarterly EPS}}{\text{standardization variable}}$$

where the standardization variable is the standard error of the estimate.

Q: Given a negative earnings surprise, does an investor have an opportunity to buy shortly after the stock drops?

17.5.3 The earnings game

Thus far we have shown that investors need to be cognizant of (1) how to obtain estimates, (2) the [in]accuracy of estimates, and (3) the impacts of earnings surprises. The earnings game is as follows:

1. analysts estimate (guess) earnings for each quarter

2. the company provides "guidance"

3. the "guidance" number is a factor in the *consensus estimate*

4. actual earnings come out different from estimates

5. some "whisper" estimates also float around just prior to announcements

Apparently Warren Buffet has argued that companies should not provide guidance. Why? May consider using sales growth estimates as well.

17.6 P/E ratio

Intriguing question: What are the reasons for cross-sectional differences in P/E ratios?

1. Consider which P/E ratio is being used. Is it based on last year's reported earnings, trailing 12-month earnings, this year's expected earnings, next year's expected earnings, etc.

2. Consider the determinants of the P/E ratio. Recall from chapter 10:

$$P/E = \frac{D_1/E_1}{k - g}$$

so there are three factors that are company specific:

   (a) the dividend payout ratio D_1/E_1
   (b) the required rate of return k
   (c) the expected growth rate in dividends g

Common Stock Analysis (chapter 11 10e/11e)

18.1 Key concepts

1. Analyze pros and cons of passive approach

2. Evaluate well-known active strategies

3. Differentiate between technical analysis and fundamental analysis

18.2 Global perspective

According to the text, one should invest 10% to 20% in foreign markets. No more than 5% in emerging markets. For perspective, look the following YTD returns for various indexes from pulled from the 2008.08.08 Wall Street Journal.

Index	Return (%)
S&P500	-13.8
Small Cap 600	-5.0
MSCI EAFE	-16.9
Venezuela	4.2
China 600	-47.0

18.3   Important issues involving common stock

18.3.1   Impact of overall market

Aggregate market movements remain the largest single factor in explaining fluctuations in individual stock prices and stock portfolios. I.e., in any multi-factor APT type analysis, market risk premium is most significant. This also applies to foreign markets.

18.3.2   Required rate of return

It is important to be aware that the required rates of return changes over time due to:

1. Changes inflationary expectations - inflation premium is a component of R_F

2. Changes in risk premiums - Investor pessimism

18.4   Building stock portfolios

What is the separation theorem? Two step process to building portfolios:

1. Asset allocation

2. Security selection

18.5   The passive strategy

If the market is "efficient enough," to impound all available information into prices quickly and accurately, no active strategy should outperform on a *risk adjusted return basis*. Advantages of passive strategy:

1. Saves analysis time - can spend your time actually making money

2. Minimizes transaction costs (fewer trades, buy-and-hold)

3. Tax efficiency

4. Index funds outperform 70% of all actively managed funds. What about the 30% that did outperform Index funds? The book does not mention tax-adjusted or fee-adjusted returns.

5. Bonus: also, there is no way to know in advance which actively manage funds will be in the winning 30%.

18.6 The active strategy

Pursuit of an active strategy *assumes* that a single or small group of investors posses some advantage relative to other market participants (read: lack of humility[1]). For example,

1. Superior analytical skills

2. Superior judgement

3. Superior information - information others do not have

4. Ability and willingness to do what other investors (in particular institutions) are unable to do.

18.6.1 Security selection

A goal of an active strategists: selection of individual stocks with superior risk-return characteristics.

18.6.1.1 Importance

Pick the right ones - you win. Pick the wrong ones - you lose. Peter lynch values the company more than the industry. McEnally and Todd (1992):

- if you confined your selection to stocks in the highest quartile you would have largely avoided losing years, and even the bad years would have had modest losses.

- If you confined your selection to lowest quartile, results were negative 55% of the time, and 25% of the time the best stocks would have lost money despite favorable market conditions

All this is saying is that rewards can be high, but so is the risk and negative consequences of poor selection.

---

[1] modest view of ones importance, humbleness

18.6.1.2   Role of security analysts

There are two types of analysts:

Sell-side cover stocks and make recommendations to *individual* investors. For example, Value Line and Standard and Poor's.

Buy-side employed by financial firms to search for securities for their *firm* to purchase.

Input   What do analysts base their recommendations on?

1. Presentations from the firm's top management

2. Annual reports

3. Quarterly reports

4. Historical data

Output   Analysts reports typically include company bio, *earnings estimates*, buy/hold/sell recommendations.

Not surprisingly, analysts' estimates have not become more accurate even with advanced technology and analysis techniques. Why? Nevertheless, their influence is hardly negligible. See Figure 11-3 (10e) or Figure 11-2 (11e) for what I call the "self-fulfilling prophecy effect."

Keep in mind, in the absence of moral conviction and the presence of incentives to cheat, people will cheat. Many lawsuits over analysts reports have occurred.

18.6.2   Sector Rotation

Another important "angle" of active strategies is sector rotation. Here we are looking for sectors that expected to be in favor in the next period. Sectors can be considered large groups:

1. interest sensitive stocks (financial companies)

2. Consumer durables (washing machines, cars (except GM), etc.)

3. Capital goods (production equipment)

4. Defensive stocks (food, alcohol and tobacco, pharmaceuticals)

Sector selection requires an understanding of economic business cycles, credit conditions, political environment, etc. There are over 600+ sector funds to facilitate sector selection.

Momentum There is some evidence of a 3 to 12 month momentum on U.S. stocks. See my dissertation for more information. :)

18.6.3 Market timing

Market timing involves varying portfolio weights in attempts to earn excess returns (in excess of what? - what is expected for given level of risk). In essence, you are looking to determine the right and wrong times to be in the market (or a particular security). The ol' buy-low and sell-high (but how do you determine what is low and what is high?). Another term for this is *technical analysis*. There is little evidence of market timing ability.

Sharpe 1975 Switching between stocks and cash equivalents could enhance returns but you need to be right 70% of the time

Bauer and Dahlquist 2001 Need to be right 66% of the time to outperform choices made by flipping a coin. Also, accuracy requirements increases with holding period.

Charles Ellis 1998 *"Market timing is a wicked idea. Don't try it ever."*[2]

See Figure 11-4 (10e) or Figure 11-3 (11e) for an interesting perspective on trying to time the market:

18.6.4 Rational markets and active strategies

Is the market efficient? Are securities fairly priced? Will active strategy X consistently beat the market? Be careful and do not forget to include three unavoidable costs of active strategies:

1. Time investment

2. taxes

3. transaction costs

---

[2]there is biblical support for this as well - do not be greedy for gain, gather little by little, etc.

18.7   Approaches for analyzing and selecting stocks

Technical analysis   The search for identifiable and recurring stock price patterns. Examples MACD, cup and handle, support/resistance/breakout, momentum, etc.

Fundamental analysis   The study of a stock's value using basic data such as earnings, sales, risk, and so forth.

Behavioral finance   The study of investment behavior based on the belief that investors may act irrationally. Interesting field... Should one be deemed irrational if their utility function (shape of indifference curve) changes? Remember:

1. "At the end of the day" stocks are worth what people pay for them

2. Have humility - if you find a pattern or fundamental value, do not assume the other 200 million investors did not see it

3. do not forget time, taxes, and transaction costs

18.7.1   Fundamental analysis framework

18.7.1.1   Bottom up approach

Porter's five forces   concerned with the impacts of suppliers, customers, barriers to entry, substitute products, and competition.

SWOT analysis   Strengths, weaknesses, opportunities, and threats.

Miscellaneous   Does growth vs. value matter much anymore? See Box 11-1 on page 306. Has anyone read this?

18.7.1.2   Top down approach

This is the approach recommended by the book

Economy/market   Is a recession likely? What is the outlook for corporate profits? 25 to 50% of earnings variability is attributable to the overall economy (including an industry effect). Is it favorable to invest in stocks at this time?

Industry/Sector analysis Industry effects are the second most influential factor affecting stock return variability. If in recession → avoid heavy goods. Inflationary period → avoid utilities. Watch for "hot" industries - synthetic fuels, genetic engineering, oil, defense.

company analysis Who has the better P/E ratio? Which company has better ROA, ROE, ROI? Which company has better earnings prospects?

NINETEEN

Bonds Analysis (chapter 18 10e/11e)

19.1 Key concepts

- Reasons to buy bonds

- Managing a bond portfolio

- Term structure of interest rates

- Passive and active bond portfolio strategies

- Conservative / aggressive investor perspectives on bond portfolio construction

19.2 Why buy bonds

- Hold to maturity: Offer a steady stream of interest income sans default of the issuer

- Trade: seek to capitalize on bond price movement

- Diversify: stable positive income when stocks are tanking

19.2.1 Why buy foreign bonds

- May offer higher return than domestic bonds at a given point in time

- Diversification

- Speculators: may try to capitalize on expected exchange rate fluctuations (but you are also exposed to an additional source of risk: currency risk)

19.3   Managing a bond portfolio

19.3.1   Understanding the bond market

1. Weak economy $\rightarrow$ (i) fewer opportunities in equity markets and (ii) lower interest rates to boost investment $\rightarrow$ more money in bonds (bond prices rise)

2. Expected increase in inflation $\rightarrow$ lower bond prices (higher bond yields)

3. *Fortune* magazine: a 1.5% rise in interest rates in 1994 translated into $600 billion loss on U.S. bonds and a possible $1.5 trillion loss worldwide.

4. Global factors: factors that increase or decrease demand for U.S. bonds:

   (a) Strengthening dollar $\rightarrow$ increased demand of dollar-denominated assets

   (b) Crises in other countries $\rightarrow$ increase demand of "safer" U.S. investments

19.3.2   Term structure of interest rates

Definition. *Term structure of interest rates* - The relationship between TTM and YTM *for a particular category* of bonds.

Definition. *Yield curve* - A graphical depiction of the term structure of interest rates

Definition. *Forward Rates* - Unobservable rates expected to prevail in the future. E.g.., the rate of a 1 year bond, 2 years from now.

Expectations theory Long-term rate of interest is equal to the average of short-term rates that are expected to prevail over the long-term period. E.g., the 10 year rate is equivalent to holding 10 1-year bonds in succession based on the *expected* 1 year rates.

For expositional[1] purposes let

$$_t R_n = \text{yield known at time } t \text{ of bond with } n \text{ periods to maturity}$$
$$_{t+s} r_n = \text{expected yield } s \text{ periods from today for } n \text{ period bond}$$
$$= \text{i.e., the forward rate}$$

Therefore the expectations theory allows you to explain the current z year bond rate using expected 1-year rates:

$$_t R_z = \left(\prod_{i=0}^{z-1} (1 +_{t+i} r_1) \right)^{1/z} - 1.0 \tag{19.1}$$

Note: $_t r_1 =_t R_1$ expectation of one year rate for today *is* the one year rate for today.

An example...   Q: So, where do forward rates come from?   A couple ways to calculate forward rates using quoted *zero coupon* bond prices and rates.

Method 1   use quoted interest rates:

$$R_{forward} = \frac{R_2 T_2 - R_1 T_1}{T_2 - T_1} \tag{19.2}$$

Method 2   Use quoted bond prices:

$$R_{forward} = \frac{1}{T_2 - T_1} \left(\frac{P_1 - P_2}{P_2} \right) \tag{19.3}$$

where

$$T_i = \text{maturity } i \text{ (years)}$$
$$P_i = \text{current price of bond with maturity of } T_i$$
$$R_{forward} = \text{rate from period } T_i \text{ to } T_j \text{ where } j > i$$

Liquidity preference theory Expectations theory plus liquidity (risk) premiums, i.e., the premium received for loaning money for a longer time period.

---

[1] explanation of theory

Market segmentation theory Investors confine their activities to specific maturities and can not be induced to change maturities. The yield curve shape is determined by supply and demand in each maturity.

Preferred habitat theory Similar to market segmentation but investors *can* be induced to change maturities with appropriate compensation.

Life insurance companies tend to have longer maturity bonds whereas banks tend to have shorter term maturities. Why? Not every policy holder is going to die simultaneously so liquidity is not much of a concern for life insurance policies. Banks need to have cash on hand for demand deposits or to make loans.

Note these are all theories which attempt to explain the term structure of interest rates. All of the theories mentioned here point towards an upward sloping yield curve.

Using the yield curve The slope of the yield has *some* predictive power according to a publication in the top finance journal: Estralla and Hardouvelis (1991), Journal of Finance.

1. Positive slope yield curve → future increase in real economic activity

2. Flattening or inverted yield curve → precedes a recession. Evidence:

   (a) All six recessions were preceded by an inverted yield curve (however one inverted curve was not followed by a recession)

   (b) Curve was inverted in April 2000

Figure 19.1 provides an example of recent yield curves.[2]:

Figure 19.2 is an illustration of the relationship between yield curve slopes and market performance.

19.3.3   Yield spreads

Definition. *Yield spread* - The relationship between the bond yield and particular features of bonds.

Keep in mind a comparison of two identical bonds with the only difference being...

---

[2]Direct from the U.S. Treasury www.ustreas.gov

Figure 19.1: Sample yield curves

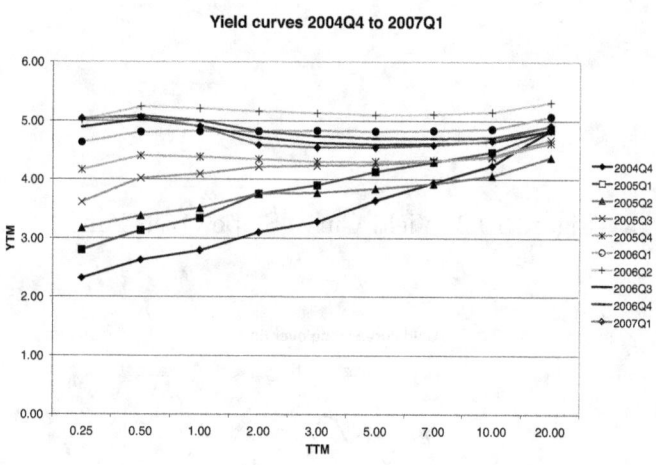

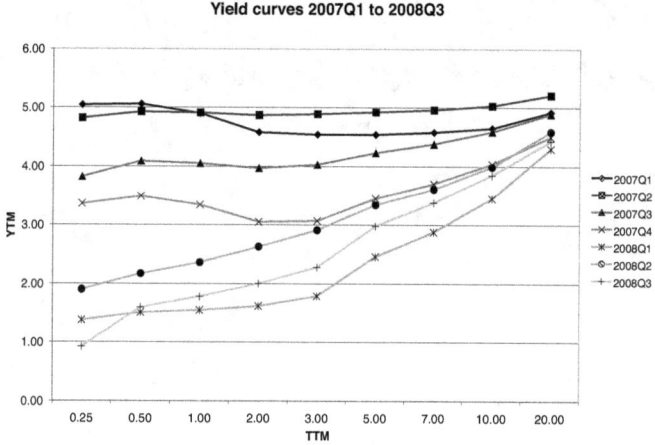

Figure 19.2: Yield Curve Slope Over Time

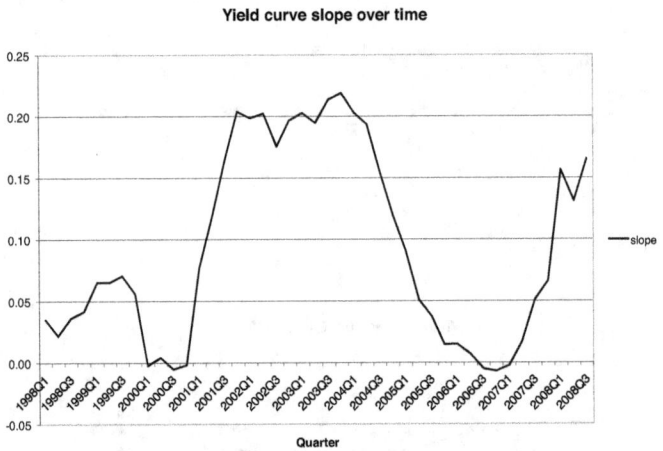

1. Quality: lower rated bonds should have a higher yield than higher rated bonds, *ceratis paribus*. You must be compensated for risk.

2. Callability: Bonds that are callable should have higher yields than identical non-callable bonds. If the bond is called, it can only be replaced with a lower YTM bond. Q: Why?

3. Coupon rate: Lower coupon $\rightarrow$ more gains in the form of price appreciation $\rightarrow$ capital gains tax treatment vs. interest tax treatment

4. Marketability (liquidity): Some bonds can be sold more readily than others. The less marketable, the higher the YTM. Must be compensated for liquidity risk.

5. Country / exchange rate risk

Other factors

1. Level of interest rates: higher interest rates $\rightarrow$ higher risk premiums (and subsequent yield spreads)

2. Time: yield spreads widen during recessions because investors are more risk averse and require increased compensation for risk.

Understanding yield spread as investor   Q: What can cause the spread between corporate bonds and US treasuries to rise?

1. Accounting debacles: Worldcom, enron, tyco

2. Litigation: Halliburton involved in asbestos exposure

3. Excessive debt levels

4. Weak earnings

GM high-yield (sounds like junk) bonds may be a good investment if you believe they will ultimately turn things around. If they do, the yield spreads will lower and the price of the GM bonds you purchased will rise.

19.4   Bond strategies

19.4.1   Passive management strategies

1. Buy and hold: *Carefully* choose a portfolio of bonds and do not attempt to trade them in search of higher returns.

2. Laddering: a form of buy and hold. If you have $100,000, put $20k in each of a 1, 2, 3, 4, and 5 year bond. If interest rates rise, you will be able to reinvest your "large" coupons into "cheap" bonds. If interest rates decline, you will be to receive *some* relatively large coupons. Think of it as dollar cost averaging in the bond space.

3. Indexing: Of course, the evidence suggests passive index bond funds outperform actively managed bond funds. For instance, the *Vangurad Total Bond Market Index* has an expense ratio of 0.2 percent and outperformed 89% of actively managed bond funds over the period 1996 to 1998

19.4.2   Immunization

The goal of immunization is to achieve a pre-specified rate of return over a selected period of time. To begin, consider two components of interest rate risk:

1. Price risk: from the inverse relationship between bond prices and YTM

2. Reinvestment rate risk: from the uncertainty at which future coupons can be reinvested.

Notice how these components move in opposite directions:

- rise in interest rates: reinvestment rates rise (good), prices of bonds you own decline (bad)

- decline in interest rates: reinvestment rates decline (bad), prices of bonds you own rise (good)

19.4.3   Immunization example

Setup   Current YTM is 7.9%. Therefore, under the reinvestment rate assumption of YTM, an investor expects a return of $(1.079)^5$, or $1.46254 per dollar invested today. Further suppose the following:

- Bond A can be purchased with a maturity date of year 5, 7.9% coupon, and 7.9% YTM

- Bond B can be purchased with a maturity date of year **6**, 7.9% coupon, 7.9% YTM and duration of 5 years

19.4.4 Active management strategies

Active management strategy Seek additional returns through trading activity. The primary tools used in the additional return search include (1) forecasting interest rate changes and (2) identifying relative mis-pricings. Note, whenever we talk about "mis-pricings" we are talking about market inefficiency. Keep in mind transaction costs and taxes before jumping to the conclusion markets are inefficient.

Forecasting changes in interest rates Why is this important to do when following an active management strategy? Due to the bond price-interest rate relationship. How accurate and consistent are forecasts? Not. Duration plays an important role (don't have to look at *both* YTM and coupon payment). You can also use bond swaps or interest-rate futures contracts.

Identifying mispricings among securities Maybe GM is mis-priced now? Example 18-9 of the book: in late 1998, $YTM_{conv} = YTM_{regular}$ when it should be greater for the additional risk. This was due to unusual selling of convertibles by hedge funds to raise cash.

19.5 Building a fixed-income portfolio

Match investor's risk/return and time horizon with bond portfolio. Remember, you seek to maximize return for a given level of risk (or, alternatively, minimize risk for a given level of return). This is accomplished by diversification with consideration given to (1) Quality, (2) Callability, (3) liquidity, (4) duration, and (5) international investment.

TWENTY

Technical Analysis (chapter 16 10e/11e)

20.1 Key concepts

1. Difference between technical and fundamental analysis

2. Evaluate most of the technical analysis techniques

3. Decide what role, if any, should technical analysis play in your own investing

20.2 What is technical analysis

Technical analysis The use of specific market data for analysis of both aggregate stock prices and individual stock prices.

Market data Price and volume information for stocks or indexes

Three points of technical analysis:

1. does not involve fundamental data such as earnings, sales, growth rates, or government regulations. Rather it focuses on aggregate market movements, industry averages, and the stock itself.

2. Focus is to identify trends

3. asses overall situation of stocks by analyzing technical indicators such as market sentiment and momentum

Part IV

Derivative Securities

TWENTYONE

Options (chapter 19 10e/11e)

21.1 Key concepts

- Understand why investors use options

- Available option alternatives

- Option market operation

- Basic option strategies

- Option valuation

21.2 Why have derivative securities?

1. They allow for investors to construct otherwise unavailable payoff patterns - market "completeness"

2. Provide risk management

3. Substitute for trading barrels of oil - contributes to gambling (see discussion of futures in Chapter 20)

4. To permit speculation. Q: Do you think we need more of this?

21.3   Introduction

Option Contracts which give the owner the right (option) to buy or sell the underlying asset within some time frame. The seller of the option has an *obligation* to buy or sell within some timeframe.

Call option An option to buy a stock at a stated (strike) price within a specified period of time

Put option An option to sell a stock a stated (strike) price within a specified timeframe.

- Q: When you buy a call, what are you anticipating? When you buy a put?

- Q: How about writing a call? (obligation to buy) How about writing a put? (obligation to sell).

Okay, so you have some reason to believe to the stock will rise or fall. Why not just buy the stock or sell it short?

1. Expands the opportunity set.

2. Takes less initial investment. Suppose you believe Google is going to go up even more. You don't have $400 × 100 shares = $40,000 to invest. You do have $59 × 100 = $5,900 to invest in a January 2007 $410 call option. This speaks to market "completeness" - but don't forget capitalism: wealthy investors pay lower transaction fees and can still buy more options.

3. Options provide leverage. More leverage than fully margined stock transactions. Would need to get into the bowels of option valuation to demonstrate this.

4. Index options allow you to participate in market *movements*.

21.4   Understanding options

21.4.1   Options terminology

Exercise/strike price - The per-share price at which the common stock is purchased/sold.

Expiration date Date an option expires

Option premium The cost of the option. $f[K, \sigma, T, S_0]$

LEAPS Long-Term Equity Anticipation Securities - options on individual securities with expiration dates up to two years. There are about 450 stocks (all expire in January) and several indexes (all expire in December).

21.4.2 The mechanics of trading

The options exchanges There are five option exchanges in the U.S.: CBOE (Chicago), ASE (?), PhSE (Philadelphia), PaSE (Pacific), and ISE (International Securities Exchange in NY). Interesting note: ISE began in May 2000 as an all electronic network. More efficiency + competition = lower costs, lower spreads, quicker execution. Law of one price.

Options Clearing Corporation Functions as an intermediary between buyers and sellers. Once brokers negotiate price on the floor (recall, these are exchanges), they deal with the OCC. The OCC ensures contract obligations will be met. Not quite sure how the OCC is compensated.

21.5 Basic option payoffs

Keep in mind: buy low / sell high.

21.5.1 Calls (buy low)

Call option *buyer* (long) payoff:

$$PO = \begin{cases} S_T - E & \text{if} \quad S_T > E \\ 0 & \text{if} \quad S_T \leq E \end{cases} \tag{21.1}$$

Note: the *profit* $\Pi = PO - c$. Call option *writer/seller* (short) payoff:

$$PO = \begin{cases} -(S_T - E) & \text{if} \quad S_T > E \\ 0 & \text{if} \quad S_T \leq E \end{cases} \tag{21.2}$$

Note: the profit $\Pi = PO + c$.

Example $S_0 = 48$, $E = 50$, call premium $= c = 4$ (per share). See Figure 19-2 (10e,11e) and Figure 19-3 (10e,11e).

21.5.2   Puts (sell high)

Put option *buyer* (long) payoff:

$$PO = \begin{cases} 0 & \text{if } S_T \geq E \\ E - S_T & \text{if } S_T < E \end{cases} \tag{21.3}$$

Note: the profit $\Pi = PO - p$. Put option *writer/seller* (short) payoff:

$$PO = \begin{cases} 0 & \text{if } S_T \geq E \\ -(E - S_T) & \text{if } S_T < E \end{cases} \tag{21.4}$$

Note: the profit $\Pi = PO + p$. See Figure 19-4 (10e, 11e) and Figure 19-5 (10e, 11e) .

21.5.3   Putting puts and calls together

Table 21.1: The long and short of call and put

	Call	Put
Buyer (long position)	option to buy	option to sell
Seller (short position)	obligation to sell	obligation to buy

21.6   Basic option strategies

Hedge Derivative strategy to reduce (or eliminate risk) by taking a position in the underlying asset.

Covered call Long position in stock, sell (short position) call. The payoff is:

$$PO = \begin{cases} E & \text{if } S_T > E \quad \text{option is exercised} \\ S_T & \text{if } S_T \leq E \quad \text{option not exercised} \end{cases} \tag{21.5}$$

An example...   See Figure 19-7 (10e, 11e)
Q: What observations can be made from the graph?

Protective put Long position in stock, buy (long position) put. Payoff is

$$PO = \begin{cases} S_T & \text{if} \quad S_T \geq E \quad \text{option not exercised} \\ E & \text{if} \quad S_T < E \quad \text{option is exercised} \end{cases} \tag{21.6}$$

Q: Why might one interpret a covered call as pretty useless and a protective put a good idea, if you already own the stock?

Portfolio insurance A technique to lock in returns. When using protective-puts for insurance, keep in mind two costs:

1. the cost of the option itself

2. the opportunity cost (money spent on option could have gained if market went up)

A real-world example...

21.7 Option valuation

21.7.1 Intrinsic and time values

The cost of an option includes the intrinsic and time value:

$$\text{option price} = \text{intrinsic value} + \text{time value} \tag{21.7}$$

For example, for a call option:

$$\text{intrinsic value}_{\text{call}} = \max[S_0 - E, 0] \tag{21.8}$$

The time value can be obtained from the quoted option price and the intrinsic value. Note the time value will approach zero as expiration approaches, but the intrinsic value does not, otherwise arbitrage opportunities would exist. These leads to two observations:

- If holder of call option wishes to purchase stock, the investor will sell the option *then* buy the stock. Why? Selling the option enables realization of the *time value*.

- This leads to an intuitive explanation why American calls and European calls have the same value[1]: you will not exercise an American option early because you would lose the time value.

---

[1] by the way, the *payoff* at expiration is identical for both types

21.7.2   Option price boundaries

The maximum price for a call option is obvious: it can not cost more than the stock itself. Otherwise, you would just buy the stock. What about the minimum? Consider the value at the instant before expiration (i.e., when the time value is zero). At this point the option value is simply the intrinsic value ($\max[S_T - E, 0]$) represented by the lower graph of pane (c). Panel (d) is more easily describable using the Black-Scholes formula. See Figure 19-4 (10e, 11e).

21.7.3   Black-Scholes model

Fisher Black and Myron Scholes developed a model to value call options on *non-dividend* paying stocks:

$$c = S_0 N[d_1] - Ke^{-rt} N[d_2] \tag{21.9}$$

where

$$c = \text{price of call option (option premium)}$$
$$S_0 = \text{current market price of underlying common stock}$$
$$N[\cdot] = \text{cumulative density function}$$
$$K = \text{exercise (strike) price}$$
$$e = \text{base of natural logarithms (2.71828)}$$
$$r = \text{continuously compounded risk-free rate of interest}$$
$$= \text{instantaneous risk free rate}$$
$$t = \text{time before expiration (in years)}$$

d_i are found by solving the following equations:

$$d_1 = \frac{\ln[S_0/K] + (r + \sigma^2/2)t}{\sigma\sqrt{t}}$$
$$d_2 = d_1 - \sigma\sqrt{t}$$

An example...

21.7.4   Put option valuation

What we just calculated was a *call* option value. What about the value of a *put* option? One method is to apply the put-call parity theorem:

Theorem. PUT-CALL PARITY - *The relationship between put and call prices such that no arbitrage opportunities exist.*

$$p + S_0 = Ke^{-rt} + c \qquad\qquad (21.10)$$

Proof. Construct two portfolios   □

Table 21.2: Put-call parity theorem proof

	Portfolio A	Portfolio B
action	buy put, buy stock	buy call, invest PV of K
cost	$p + S_0$	$c + Ke^{-rt}$
payoff at expiration	PO_A	PO_B

For portfolio A, if $S_T \leq K$, you will exercise your put option and *sell high* at K. If $S_T > K$ you will *not* exercise the put option for if you did you would be selling low. For portfolio B, $S_T \leq K$, you will *not buy high* at K, therefore you will be left with K. If $S_T > K$, you will *buy low* at K and have an asset worth S_T. Therefore

$$PO_A = PO_B = \begin{cases} K & S_T \leq K \\ S_T & S_T > K \end{cases}$$

An example ... Compute value of put option using (21.10).

21.7.5   Option value factors

See Table 19-1 (10e, 11e) .

All of these can be readily seen through comparative statics applied to (21.9) and (21.10).

21.7.6   Hedge ratios

Definition. The ratio of options written (sold, obligation to sell stock in future) to shares of stock held long in a risk-less portfolio.

This is also commonly referred to as **delta**, the change in option price for $1 change in price of stock. In (21.9), $N[d_1]$ is the *hedge ratio* (or *delta*). Note the hedge ratio will *always* be less than one. Therefore, dollar movements option prices are smaller than dollar movements in the underlying stocks. However, the *percentage* change for an option price is generally larger than the percentage price change on the stock.

21.7.7   Using the Black-Scholes model

The B-S model makes several assumptions:

1. Instantaneous interest rates are constant

2. Volatility is constant over time

3. no dividends (note, when dividends are paid, the stock price declines)

4. stock price changes follow a log-normal distribution

What does all this mean? Running the numbers and finding an undervalued option is not necessarily evidence of an arbitrage opportunity.

21.8   Stock-index options

21.8.1   The basics

- Became available in 2001

- Behave like stock options except the underlying asset, the stock index, is not bought or sold.

- When exercised, a cash settlement equal to the difference of the closing index price and strike price multiplied by a specified dollar amount.

21.8.2   Strategies

An example that illustrates the leverage advantage of index options, or options in general.

TWENTYTWO

Futures (chapter 20 10e/11e)

22.1 Key concepts

1. Why futures markets exist

2. Distinction between futures an forward contracts

3. Available futures contracts

4. Futures-based strategies

22.2 Understanding futures markets

- Futures have been described as a "financial innovation"

- Warning: Credit-Default-Swaps were also described as "financial innovations"

- Futures allow for speculation: do we really need more speculation?[1]

22.2.1 Why futures markets?

First, a couple definitions:

Spot market market for immediate delivery at *spot price*

---

[1]for pleasure reading, look for the book entitled "The intelligent investor" by Benjamin Graham for a contrast between *investors* and *speculators*

Forward market market for delivery in the future at *forward price*

Example

- Josten's is concerned the price of gold will increase before May of next year when people purchase graduation rings

- Why have a futures contract: To lock in a price today for gold purchased in May to make the rings.

- Why not: price of gold may go down in the future and Josten's would be obligated to pay more if they entered into a forward/futures contract

- Q: As a diversified investor, do you want a corporation to concern themselves about forward/futures contracts?

22.2.2   Forward vs. future

Forward contract an agreement between to parties to buy (sell) something in the future at a specified price. No cost for a forward contract.

Futures contract standardized (by size, delivery date, quality) forward contract that is traded. Since it is traded, it has a price.

Regarding credit risk:

- Forward contracts have credit risk since either party can default (lack of payment and/or delivery)

- Futures contracts do not have credit risk since "performance is ensured" by the Commodity Futures Trading Commission (CFTC)

- Regulation of futures markets

  - Not regulated by SEC since futures are not securities

  - Regulation duties shared by (1) government agency - the CFTC and (2) self-regulating body (National Futures Association)[2]

---

[2]How may of you believe self-regulation is the answer?

22.2.3   Futures markets

- Futures exchanges are non-profit associations financed by membership dues and service fees

- Parties settle contracts with the clearinghouse (a separate corporation), not each other

- Two functions of futures markets

    1. Price discovery: can asses the market's current expectation of future prices by looking at the prices of futures contracts
    2. Risk transfer: Josten's passes on risk to speculator

- Two categories of futures markets

    1. Commodities: food, oil, wood, etc.
    2. Financials: stock indexes, interest rates, foreign currency, etc.

- Europe has consolidated futures markets

- Japan banned financial futures until 1985. Q: Why?

22.3   Mechanics of futures trading

22.3.1   Basic procedures

- No money is exchanged when the contract is negotiated (originated, initially entered)

- Short position: agreement to sell an asset in at a specified future date at a specified price

- Long position: agreement to purchase an asset at a specified future date at a specified price

- In contrast, an option is a *exercisable right* to buy or sell whereas a futures contract is an agreement (or obligation) to buy or sell

- The futures obligation is resolved by one of two ways:

1. Offset: liquidation of a futures position by an offsetting transaction (we will see an example shortly)

2. Delivery

- 95% of futures contracts are settled by offset. Q: Why?

- Futures exchanges establish price fluctuation limits. E.g., corn:

  1. minimum transaction $\Delta P = 12.50$ per contract

  2. maximum daily $\Delta P = 500$ per contract

- Does limit (1) remind you of decimalization? Q: What is the advantage to establishing minimum price change limits?

22.3.2   Margin

- Unlike stocks and stock options, *margin* in the context of futures contracts is *not* borrowed money

- Futures margin: the earnest money deposit made by a transactor to ensure the completion of a contract

- Initial margin: the part of a transactions value a customer must pay to initiate the transaction, with the remainder borrowed

- Initial margin is typically small (6% of contract value)

- Maintenance margin: percentage of a security's value that must be on hand at all times as equity

- Margin call: demand from the broker for additional cash or securities as a result of actual margin falling below the maintenance margin. The specific amount request must bring the account back to the initial margin standing.

- Marked to market: the daily posting of all profits and losses on a contract to each account

22.4 Financial futures example

DJIA Stock-Index future:

- Contract multiplier: $CM = \$10$

- value of contract: $V = CM \times DJIA$ (e.g., $\$10 \times 10,000 = \$100,000$)

- Seller of contract (short position): agrees to sell $10 times the *current* index value on the expiration date $\to$ betting index will decline from current level

- Buyer of contract (long position): agrees to buy $10 times the *current* index value on the expiration date $\to$ betting index will increase from current level

- At expiration, the winner of the bet receives $|DJIA_T - DJIA_0| \times \$10$ from the loser$\to$ zero-sum game

- Example with $DJIA_0 = 10,000$, initial margin $= \$7,000$; and maintenance margin $= \$3,000$

	Buyer (long)	Seller (short)
Day 0: Initial contract, $DJIA_0 = 10,000$		
current equity	$7,000	$7,000
Day 1, 75 point drop in DJIA $DJIA_1 = 10,000 - 75 = 9,925$		
gain (loss)	(750)	750
current equity	$6,250	$7,750
Day 14: DJIA rises to $DJIA_{14} = 10,400$, a 400 point rise		
gain (loss)	$4,000	($4,000)
current equity	$11,000	$3,000
withdrawable excess equity	$4,000	
margin call		$4,000

- A few things to point out regarding this example

  1. Another interpretation of Day 14: The buyer buys at the 10,000 'rate' and the seller sells at the 10,000 'rate' which is the futures contractual agreement. Thus, the buyer buys low at 10,000 to meet the futures contract obligation and sells high at 10,400 to make a profit. Meanwhile, the seller buys high at 10,400 and sells low 10,000 to meet the futures contract obligation and incurs a loss.

2. The "current equity" is obtained by "marking to market" each day

3. The expiration date of this futures contract is still some point in the future

4. Q: Why is the buyer able to withdraw $4,000?

5. Q: Why must the seller pony up another $4,000?

6. To illustrate the zero-sum game nature, redo the calculations if the DJIA drops to 9,500 on day 15!

22.5   Using futures contracts

22.5.1   Hedgers

- The hedged position reduces (but not necessarily *eliminates*) volatility while maintaining the same expected return. See Figure 20-1 (10e, 11e).

- An example with real data...

- The Josten's case was an example of a **long hedge**: A transaction where the asset is currently not held but futures are purchased to lock in current prices

- A farmer with corn to sell in one month who *sells* a futures contract has entered a **short hedge** a transaction involving the sale of futures while holding the asset.

22.5.2   Hedging with interest rate futures

- The price of interest rate futures contracts move opposite of interest rates

- expect rates to rise: sell (short) futures contract. Q: Why?

- expect rates to decline: buy (long) futures contract. Q: Why?

22.5.3   Speculators

- Do not have nor plan to have the physical commodity

- Deemed "essential" because the assume the unwanted risk of hedgers

- Q: Why speculate with futures as opposed to the underlying instrument?

- Small investors are better off using futures for hedging, not speculating

22.6 Stocks, options, and single-stock futures

A [very] brief comparison.

	Stocks	SSFs	Options
payoff profile	linear	linear	non-linear
return distribution	[log] normal	[log] normal	truncated
margin	finance trans.	earnest money	finance trans.